PRAISE FOR
KINKY FRIEDMAN

"The new Mark Twain."

—*Southern Living*

"The Mother Teresa of literature."

—Willie Nelson

"A Texas legend."

—George W. Bush

"Sometimes he's outrageous. Most of the time, he's outrageously funny."

—*People*

"Spreads more joy than Ross Perot's ears."

—Molly Ivins

"[Friedman] is in his own genre. His prose can range from the purely poetic to the pornographic to the deeply philosophical, quite often in the same sentence. He is a wordsmith of the first order."

—Fannie Flagg,
The New York Times Book Review

"I've now read all your books. More, please. I *really* need the laughs."

—President William Jefferson Clinton

St. Martin's Griffin
New York

TEXAS HOLD 'EM

HOW I WAS BORN IN A MANGER, DIED IN THE SADDLE,
AND CAME BACK AS A HORNY TOAD

KINKY FRIEDMAN

Illustrations by John Callahan

Some of the pieces of this book have appeared in different form in *Texas Monthly* and *Rolling Stone*.

Grateful acknowledgment is made to the copyright holders for permission to use material from the following copyrighted works:

Illustrations on pages xvi, 101, and 107 from *The Best of Callahan,* by John Callahan. Copyright © 2003 by John Callahan.

Illustrations on pages xxii and 176 from *Get Down!! Dog Cartoons,* by John Callahan. Copyright © 2002 by John Callahan.

Illustrations on pages 4, 10, 46, 123, 157, and 161 from *Do What He Says! He's Crazy!!!* By John Callahan. Copyright © 1992 by John Callahan.

Illustrations on pages 26, 67, and 199 from *The Night, They Say, Was Made for Love: Plus My Sexual Scrapbook,* by John Callahan. Copyright © 1993 by John Callahan.

Illustrations on pages 56, 111, and 181 from *Do Not Disturb Any Further,* by John Callahan. Copyright © 1990 by John Callahan.

Illustrations on pages 65 and 71 from *What Kind of God Would Allow a Thing Like This to Happen?!!* by John Callahan. Copyright © 1994 by John Callahan.

Illustration on page 186 from *Digesting the Child Within: And Other Cartoons to Live By,* by John Callahan. Copyright © 1991 by John Callahan.

Illustration on page 217 from *Freaks of Nature,* by John Callahan. Copyright © 1995 by John Callahan.

Illustrations on pages 15, 96, 132, and 142 courtesy of John Callahan. Copyright © 2005 by John Callahan.

www.stmartins.com

Book design by Amanda Dewey

Library of Congress Cataloging-in-Publication Data

Friedman, Kinky.
    Texas hold 'em : how I was born in a manger, died in the saddle, and came back as a horny toad / Kinky Friedman.
        p. cm.
    ISBN 0-312-33154-1 (hc)
    ISBN 0-312-33155-X (pbk)
    EAN 978-0-312-33155-9
    1. Friedman, Kinky—Homes and haunts—Texas—Humor. 2. Texas—Humor. I. Title.

PS3556.R527T49 2005
976.4'02'07—dc22

                                                                          2005042777

First St. Martin's Griffin Edition: May 2006

10 9 8 7 6 5 4 3 2 1

This book is dedicated to

Don Imus

A friend of thirty years

A kindred spirit

A childhood toboggan companion

A truth-seeking missile

A rodeo clown who saves the cowboy

CONTENTS

———————⋅———————

ACKNOWLEDGMENTS

The author wishes to extend his gratitude, which knows no bounds, to the following: Diane Reverand, editor; Regina Scarpa, assistant editor; David Vigliano, Elisa Petrini, and Andrea Somberg, agents; Sage Ferrero, Nancy Parker, and Steve "Beano" Boynton, contributors; Sally Richardson, John Murphy, John Cunningham, and all the fine folks at St. Martin's Press; Max Swafford, editor; Evan Smith and *Texas Monthly*; *Rolling Stone*; and, of course, the great John Callahan.

A MESSAGE FROM THE AUTHOR

Regarding the Artist

The art and illustrations for this book were created by the world-famous, widely syndicated, often praised, often vilified, paralyzed genius, John Callahan. How does he come up with the ideas? I told you. He's a fucking genius. But how, you might ask, does he actually draw the illustrations? I'll let Callahan tell you in his own words: "I clutch the pen between both hands in a pathetic, childlike manner that endears me to millions of conflicted fans around the world."

The author is highly gratified that the illustrations for this book are the creations of the brilliantly sick John Callahan, one of the few modern American artists worthy of the name. Callahan's work is imbued with a rare, primitive, visceral integrity that often creates in me a mild state of sexual arousal. There are a number of instances, indeed, when Callahan's art so perfectly mates with my prose that it is cause for celebration, and, perhaps quite understandably, causes me to mas-turbate like the monkey on the back of Lenny Bruce.

John Callahan also writes songs. Many people like to sing and record John's songs. He is currently at work on a new CD that contains one of my favorite Callahan tunes, "Purple Wi-noes in the Rain." As Waylon Jennings once told me, if I had a session tonight I'd cut it. Unfortunately, I haven't had a ses-sion in almost twenty-five years, unless you want to count a recent session with a large Bulgarian masseuse.

Texas Hold 'Em, liberally decorated with Callahan drop-pings, should provide an entertaining diversion for the many among us who suffer from suicidal depression and whose lives are spiraling downward into tailspins of despair. Others, suffer-ing from Attention Deficit Disorder, may find John Callahan's offerings enjoyable as well. And as for the rest of us? What the hell. Somewhere in all this horseshit there's got to be a pony.

Don't worry, he won't get far on foot.

TEXAS HOLD 'EM:
AN INTRODUCTION

———◆———

Texas Hold 'Em is more than just a card game. It deals, I believe, with that fine, forgotten art of playing a poor hand well. The literary voyage you are about to embark upon captures some of the more colorful people, pictures, and places that have populated my mind as I've wandered in the raw poetry of time. As the poet and songwriter Billy Joe Shaver once wrote: "Fenced yards ain't hold cards and like as not never will be." In other words, Texas Hold 'Em is a state of mind, a spiritual survival technique, a way of holding on to things that might just be important in this ever-changing world.

Take Willie Nelson, for instance, a man I sometimes refer to as the Hillbilly Dalai Lama. In the long run, Willie may well have more impact upon the minds of men and women than all the political leaders the Lone Star State has ever produced. I told him as much recently and his response was to inscribe to me in one of *his* books the following sentiment: "To Kinky— Thanks for taking time out in your busy schedule to honor my bus with your esteemed presence. May the breath of Allah blow out your ass. Love, Willie Nelson."

> **"Fenced yards ain't hold cards and like as not never will be."**
> —BILLY JOE SHAVER
>
> ♦
>
> **"May the breath of Allah blow out your ass."**
> —WILLIE NELSON

Willie has stayed true to the spirit of *Texas Hold 'Em* all his life, never allowing himself to get "above his raisin's" and I'm not talking about the little black boogers they grow in California. Born in the tiny town of Abbott, Texas, Willie picked cotton as a kid, yet grew up to become an inspiration to people all over the world, including the Kinkster. In fact, I told Willie once that I was very proud to be his third favorite Jew. "Your first is no doubt Jesus," I said, "and your second is probably your harmonica player, Mickey Raphael."

Willie nodded his head in agreement and, speaking in spontaneous rhyming verse, he said: "And you'll always be / number three / in my heart." As you can imagine, those words meant a lot to me.

And then, of course, there's George W. How does *Texas Hold 'Em* apply to George W., you may well inquire? Like father, like son; you may even invoke Ann Richards's memorable invective, "He was born with a silver foot in his mouth." And so he was. And Moses was born with a speech impediment. And

Abe Lincoln was born so ugly his opponents referred to him as "the gorilla." But *Texas Hold 'Em* is the great equalizer. On September 11, 2001, George W. Bush, possibly for the first time in his life, began to show the whole world how to play a poor hand well.

Somewhere between the legend and the lamppost, somewhere between the windmill and the world, somewhere between Willie and George, both chronologically and spiritually, I was born. As fate would have it, I was born into an upper-middle-class Jewish family, not poor enough to provide me the quaint, colorful background necessary for country music stardom, yet not rich enough to have a hope in hell of getting into the quaint, colorful oil business. Somehow, I managed.

> Like Jesus, I was either cursed or blessed by being born a Jew.

Like Jesus, I was either cursed or blessed by being born a Jew. Impressed by Jesus at an early age, I made it a point never to get married in my adult life, never to have a home, and never to have a job. Instead, I spent much of the time traveling about the countryside with a long-haired band of men, irritating many people. Also, like Jesus, I was a big believer in resurrection. I've had to resurrect my career on at least three or four occasions.

My latest resurrection involves my plan to run for governor in 2006, pledging, as the first Jewish governor of Texas, to reduce the speed limit to 54.95. Initially, I considered coming out against hunting, coming out against football, and then coming out against coming out. But then I started to get serious—well—at least committed to the prospect of actually becoming governor. It's always a good idea to keep a light hand on the tiller. Sometimes what starts out as a joke has a nasty little habit of sailing dangerously close to the truth. Now, running as an independent, I intend to demonstrate that even though the Texas governor does no heavy lifting, he can still do some spiritual lifting, that is, inspire people, especially young people, to get involved in the health, education, and welfare of their state.

> My latest resurrection involves my plan to run for governor in 2006, pledging, as the first Jewish governor of Texas, to reduce the speed limit to 54.95.
>
> ◆
>
> "Hang on tight, spur hard, and let 'er buck."

Whatever happens, for me, *Texas Hold 'Em* will always be the way in which I play the game of life. To me, *Texas Hold 'Em* means holding on to what is dear to you, to the things that made you who you are, always remembering that the most important things in life aren't things. There is an old cowboy philosophy of life that sums it up pretty well. The cowboy I first heard it from has long ago gone to the great round-up in the sky, but I still remember what he told me: "Hang on tight, spur hard, and let 'er buck."

—*Kinky Friedman*
November 2004

PART I

THE HUMMINGBIRD MAN

SEE KINKY RUN

Many moons ago I contemplated the rather whimsical possibility of my running for—or more accurately, taking a leisurely stroll toward—the high-and-mighty office of governor of Texas. There have been a number of interesting developments since then, and not all of them have transpired entirely within the febrile confines of my gray-matter department. There actually *does* seem to be genuine support for my candidacy. A good bit of it, unfortunately, appears to be emanating from the Bandera Home for the Bewildered.

In Washington last October, the president himself promised me that if I ran, he would be my "one-man focus group." During the same White House visit, I had a cordial meeting in a hallway with Colin Powell and later found myself in the men's

room with Donald Rumsfeld. Though neither man offered to help with my campaign, I did mention to Rummy that he was not the most famous person I'd ever wee-wee'd next to. The most famous, I told him, was Groucho Marx. Rummy told me he couldn't touch that one but that his wife had once danced with Jimmy Durante.

A few weeks later, at the Texas Book Festival, my campaign won the support of Molly Ivins after she asked me point-blank why I was running. "Why the hell not?" I replied.

"Beautiful," she said. "*That's* your campaign slogan." Any candidate for governor who has the support of both George W. and Molly can't be all bad.

Texas, as Molly pointed out, has a tradition of singing gov-

ernors. I thought back to Pappy O'Daniel's successful race for
that esteemed office in the forties. He had a band called the
Light Crust Doughboys. I had a band called the Texas Jewboys. His slogan was "Pass the biscuits, Pappy." One of my
most popular songs is, "Get Your
Biscuits in the Oven (And Your
Buns in the Bed)." The parallels
are uncanny. And then of course,
there was Ma Ferguson, the first
female governor, who said, "If
English was good enough for Jesus Christ, it's good enough for
Texas."

> "If English was good
> enough for Jesus
> Christ, it's good
> enough for Texas."
> —MA FERGUSON
>
> ◆
>
> I don't want a wife, I
> told him. I'm already
> married to Texas.

Thus, with George and Molly
aboard, I felt empowered enough
to do an interview with the *Kerrville Daily Times,* break the
news to my friend U.S. congressman Lamar Smith, and
green-light a first printing of bumper stickers that read "He
ain't Kinky. He's my governor." The Kerrville paper trum-
peted my interview on page one, the bumper stickers prolifer-
ated throughout the Hill Country faster than jackrabbits, and
Lamar suggested that the race, quixotic as it might seem,
would be a no-lose proposition. "You'll come out of this," he
predicted, "with a book, a wife, or the governorship." I don't
want a wife, I told him. I'm already married to Texas.

It was around this time that some people began asking me
if the whole thing was a joke. For some reason this rankled me
more than I'd expected. I'd always seen myself, in the words
of Billy Joe Shaver, as a serious soul nobody took seriously.

Why should they take me seriously now? But I wasn't about to retire in a petulant snit to a goat farm for sixteen years. I would tell them the truth with humor, for humor always sails dangerously close to the truth. Some things are too important to be taken seriously, I told them. The question is whether my candidacy is a joke or whether the current crop of politicians is the joke.

> **The question is whether my candidacy is a joke or whether the current crop of politicians is the joke.**

But there was a time in late November when I didn't have such a positive attitude. I paced back and forth in my log cabin, wondering if I was bound for the Governor's Mansion or the mental hospital. I was so uncertain of my chances at that dark time that if I'd been elected, I would have demanded a recount. Did I dare dream the impossible dream? Go for the long shot? Then the phone rang. The caller said he was from the *Times*. "That was some interview you guys did," I said. "What interview?" asked the guy. "Isn't this the *Kerrville Times*?" I asked. "No," he said. "It's *The New York Times*."

The *Times* story, headlined GUESS WHO WANTS TO BE GOVERNOR, ran on Saturday, November 29, a day that will live in infamy in the minds of those who wish to perpetuate the politics of the status quo. The switchboard at the ranch lit up like a Christmas tree in Las Vegas. Fielding the congratulatory calls and offers of support was a daunting task, but I tried to be as gracious as possible. I told them all I'd get back to them in about two years.

But the calls kept coming. My old pal Tom Waits offered to come down and help the campaign, as did Willie Nelson, Dwight Yoakam, Robert Duvall, Billy Bob Thornton, Jim Nabors, Jerry Jeff Walker, Lily Tomlin, and Johnny Depp. In addition to this galaxy of stars, Penn and Teller, the Las Vegas magicians, promised to come to Texas and "make the opposition disappear." Meanwhile, Craven and Nancy Green, the parents of a struggling young songwriter named Pat Green, came up to the ranch from Waco. They brought with them the Sunday *Waco Tribune-Herald,* which had carried the *New York Times* story. "It's on page one," they said excitedly, but they seemed a bit hesitant to show me. After some badgering, I got them to hand me the paper. The story was there, all right, but the Waco editors had changed the headline to read, UN- COUTH HOPEFUL EYES GOVERNORSHIP. The campaign was already getting personal.

So what kind of governor would I be? When I was in Washington, George W. asked me what my platform was. I didn't really have an answer at the time, but I've had a chance to think it over. Next time I see him, this is what I'll say: "My platform, Mr. President, is that I'm not a politician. My platform is that I'm not a bureaucrat. My platform is that I'm a writer of fiction who speaks the truth. My platform is to fight the wussification of this great state, to rise and shine and bring back the glory of Texas. My platform is, no hill to a climber. My platform is to remember that when

> My platform is to fight the wussification of this great state, to rise and shine and bring back the glory of Texas.

they went out searching for Sam Houston to try to persuade him to be the governor—and he was the greatest governor this state has ever had—rumor has it that they found him drunk, sleeping under a bridge with the Indians."

On second thought, maybe I don't really want a platform. They might try to put a trapdoor in it.

CHANGE, PARDNERS

I never thought I'd see the day when I'd miss gun racks in the back windows of pickup trucks, but I almost do. I miss the old Texas Hill Country, where Adolph Hofner and the Pearl Wranglers performed at outdoor dance halls under the stars. I miss the days when cowboy shirts never had buttons and coffee with a friend was still a dime. Many of the stubborn, dusty, weather-beaten little towns, roads, trucks, jeeps, people, and animals are gone now. If I could, I would surround this magic kingdom with the fragile, freckled arms of childhood and keep it the way I remember it.

All through the fifties, the Medina post office had a sign on the wall that read, DO NOT SPIT ON THE FLOOR. Today, of course, it would be unthinkable for anyone to spit on the floor; that would be almost as verboten as smoking. Medina is a small, dry

town in a wet county that, to paraphrase my father, has been slowly dying for more than one hundred years—that is, until now. After standing strong through droughts, fires, and floods, Medina, along with much of the heart of Texas, is finally experiencing something that may change it forever. And as Joseph Heller once warned, "Every change is for the worse."

I'm referring, of course, to the fact that the whole world seems to be moving to the Hill Country. Some folks in Kerrville are celebrating getting a Home Depot, while yuppies in Houston and Dallas are running away from home as fast as they can. Where are they going? You've got it. "They all want a home, far away from the dome where the Cowboys and drug dealers play. Trade the smog and road rage for the stars and the sage—that's what them developers say."

Texas Highway 16 from Kerrville to Bandera is one of the most beautiful drives you can take on this planet. By day, you'll travel through rolling hills, past green valleys and wooded canyons, over sparkling creeks, and under blue skies. By night, the stars will shine even brighter than all of the above. The hills protect us, and the canyons keep us cool in the summer, and the animals go about their secret business as they did before any of us were here. Yet even the natural beauty of the land registers in our consciousness only as another theme park of the modern mind.

> I miss the days when cowboy shirts never had buttons and coffee with a friend was still a dime.

There is a phenomenon that sometimes occurs around small towns like Medina that some call the "hidy sign" but I call the "Medina wave." A driver encountering another vehicle on the highway will casually, effortlessly raise his index finger from the wheel in a brief salute, acknowledging the other driver, the countryside, and life in general. The other driver, unless he's new to these parts, will respond in kind. Occurrences of the Medina wave diminish as you reach the outskirts of the bigger towns, disappearing almost completely as you travel farther, or at least that's how it used to be. With so many new people in the area, the custom is vanishing like the fast-moving tail of a comet. These days, you're just as likely to see drivers saluting each other with their middle fingers.

Like it or not, the peaceful, scenic, bucolic Hill Country is being dragged kicking and screaming into the twenty-first century. The old-timers, who once worked the land, who drove horses and carts over these hills, who still give directions by the bends of the river, now sit in little coffee shops in little towns and watch the parade of progress. The folks from the big city are escaping the madness, believing they are making a new life for themselves in the wilderness, possibly not realizing what the old-timers already know: that sooner or later, no matter where you go, you always see yourself in the rearview mirror.

Though the Hill Country has always been warm and friendly to newcomers, tradition demands that you be born here or dead before you're truly accepted. My family has owned and lived on the same ranch on the outskirts of Medina for fifty years, yet many of the locals still refer to it as the old Sweeney place. The Reverend Sweeney was a circuit preacher who lived here in 1921, drove a Model T Ford, and kept meat down in the well for refrigeration. In the twenties the Sweeneys traded the ranch for a restaurant in San Saba that went belly-up. Several years ago, five generations of Sweeney women came through on a road trip, and a lady close to ninety gave me a message to give to my octogenarian friend Earl Buckelew. She said, "Tell John Earl the little Sweeney girls came by to say hello." Rivers run deep in the Hill Country.

> "They all want a home, far away from the dome where the Cowboys and drug dealers play."

Yet some things go on as usual. Utopia has a new restaurant called Garden of Eat'n. Bandera continues to be the hell-raising Cowboy Capital of the World, with the Silver Dollar still featuring live country bands and sawdust on the floor, and the Old

Spanish Trail still serving a chicken-fried steak as big as your hat in its John Wayne Room. The cedar choppers have all but disappeared from Ingram, and the disgruntled dentists keep pouring into Hunt. Some people brag about the new Kerrville Wal-Mart, but others are just as proud of a local institution with a memorable moniker: the Butt-Holdsworth Memorial Library. And back at the Medina post office, a Volvo has just driven up with a bumper sticker that reads, "Free Tibet."

> . . . sooner or later, no matter where you go, you always see yourself in the rearview mirror.
>
> ◆
>
> [T]he neighbors asked him why his cats were always going into their garbage cans. He told them, "They wants to see the world."

And the old-timers, like old dogs in the sun, are vaguely aware of traffic jams and conservative little towns like Fredericksburg now transmogrified into shoppers' paradises. Meanwhile, in hillbilly heaven, Slim Dodson sips his coffee, remembering a time long ago when the neighbors asked him why his cats were always going into their garbage cans. He told them, "They wants to see the world." Earl Buckelew is there, too. He recalls once showing some acreage to a guy from the city who wanted to know if the land was any good for farming or livestock. "No," said Earl. "All it's good for is holding the world together."

BIG ASS TEXAS

If you haven't heard the cliché, "Everything is bigger in Texas," you need to get out more often. Seriously. Because every 5.5 seconds someone in America utters this infamous phrase, sometimes with a tone of disdain, sometimes with a hint of admiration, and sometimes in exasperation. The truth is, not everything in Texas is big—witness the forest of mature Harvard Oak trees no taller than three feet high at Monahans Sandhills State Park, or the world's smallest skyscraper in Wichita Falls. The skyscraper was planned in the early twentieth century to be 125 feet tall, but was built in inches instead of feet, leaving investors bilked out of hundreds of thousands of dollars—but a lot of things are (bigger, that is). Here's proof:

- Texas is the largest petroleum producing state in the United States. If Texas were an independent nation, it would rank as the world's fifth largest petroleum-producing country.

- The biggest airport in the United States is the Dallas/Fort Worth airport in Grapevine, Texas.

- The Dallas/Fort Worth airport is larger than New York City's Manhattan Island.

- Texas is larger than the countries of France, Belgium, Holland, Switzerland, and Luxembourg combined.

- The Six Flags Over Texas theme park is larger than Disneyland.

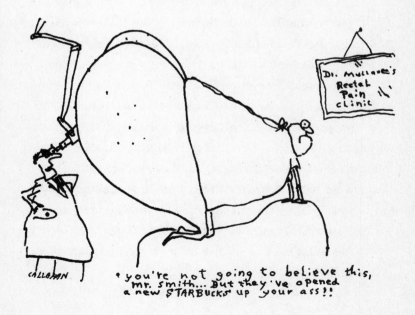

◆ The world's largest oatmeal cake was baked in Bertram, Texas, during Labor Day weekend in 1991. The thirty-three-layer cake stood more than three feet tall, weighed 333 pounds, and served 3,333 people.

◆ The largest jeans in the world are on Big Tex, at the Texas State Fair. They are Lee brand jeans, size 276 with a waist size of twenty-three feet. His boots are size seventy.

◆ The Fairmount Hotel in San Antonio was the largest building ever moved.

◆ The world's tallest masonry structure is the San Jacinto Battlefield Monument, on the Houston Ship Channel twenty-two miles southeast of Houston in Harris County. The octagonal monument was constructed between 1936 and 1939 with federal and state funds at a cost of 1.5 million dollars to commemorate the heroes of the battle of San Jacinto and all other persons who helped win the independence of Texas. It is now widely recognized as one of the best examples of modern architecture in the nation. The monument is 570 feet tall, built of reinforced concrete faced with Texas fossilized buff limestone quarried near the state Capitol at Austin. It is taller than either the Washington Monument or the Statue of Liberty. The building is crowned by a thirty-four-foot star, symbolizing the "lone star" of Texas. A reflecting pool, 1,750 feet long and 200 feet wide, mirrors the shaft from top to bottom. A 5,000-seat amphitheater behind the building offers continuous screen presentation of the battle.

- The Dallas World Aquarium is home to the world's largest freshwater aquarium tank—200,000 gallons.

- The world's largest known bat colony is in Bracken Cave near San Antonio. The largest urban colony of bats in North America is in Austin under the Congress Avenue Bridge.

- Texas has the largest road system of any state, with 184,000 lane miles.

- Texas has more counties (254) than any other state. Forty-one counties in Texas are each larger than the state of Rhode Island.

- The most famous Christmas catalog to come out of Texas is put out each year by Neiman-Marcus. In the past, such items as his-and-hers airplanes and baby elephants have been available as gift purchases. In 1976, the Neiman-Marcus catalog offered a pair of male and female American bison for 11,750 dollars. Gift wrapping was optional.

YOU KNOW YOU'RE FROM TEXAS IF . . .

You Know You're from East Texas If:

- Your television has 897 channels but you don't have indoor plumbing.

- You allow your twelve-year-old daughter to smoke at the dinner table, in front of her kids.

- You've been married and divorced five times and still have the same in-laws.

- You mow your grass and find three cars.

You Know You're from North Texas If:

- You have calfskin toilet paper in your bathroom.

- Your daughter's prom dress costs more than what most people make in a year.

- You see nothing wrong with a dog wearing a sweater.

- You bought your unborn children spots in the pre-school that sends the most kids to Harvard.

You Know You're from South Texas If:

- You own a zoot suit and consider it formal wear.

- You are proud of how high your car can hop up and down while at a standstill.

- The undercarriage of your car is so low to the ground that anything higher than a toothpick is considered a speed bump.

- You've ever been on a Chupacabra hunt.

You Know You're from West Texas If:

- You get all your power from a windmill.

- When the temperature gets under 95 degrees, you have to put on a jacket because you feel chilled.

- You encounter four other cars on a two-hundred-mile stretch of highway and complain about the traffic jam.

- Your nearest neighbor is in a different time zone.

BAND OF BROTHERS

———————◆———————

A happy childhood, I've always believed, is the worst possible preparation for life. Be that as it may, my dream as a child was to grow up to be a country music star. But if you dream of becoming a country music star as a kid, you'll invariably wind up a best-selling novelist. It's just a little trick God plays on us, like the channel swimmer drowning in the bathtub. But for me, becoming a writer has been a rather fortuitous turn of events. For one thing, I've always wanted a lifestyle that didn't require my presence. For another, I've always been somewhat ambivalent about performing and lately I've come to realize that anyone who uses the word "ambivalent" should never have been a country singer in the first place. As Joseph Heller once observed, "Nothing succeeds as planned."

With country music still in my head after I graduated from the University of Texas, I joined the Peace Corps and worked for eleven cents an hour in the jungles of Borneo. As an agricultural extension worker, my job was to help people who'd been farming successfully for more than two thousand years to improve their agricultural methods. I was supposed to distribute seeds downriver, but the Peace Corps never sent me any. Eventually, I was forced to distribute my own seed downriver, which had some rather unpleasant repercussions. Still, it was in Borneo that I wrote some of my first country songs and dreamed up the great notion of putting together a band called Kinky Friedman and the Texas Jewboys.

Several years later the Texas Jewboys became a reality, a country band with a social conscience, a demented love child of Lenny Bruce and Bob Wills. The group included four Texans: Jeff "Little Jewford" Shelby, Kenny "Snakebite" Jacobs, Thomas William "Wichita" Culpepper, and myself, Richard Kinky "Big Dick" Friedman. All of us except for Wichita were Jewish. The other original members—Billy Swan, Willie Fong Young, and Rainbow Colors—were all Texans and Jews by inspiration. There were other Texas Jewboys over the years, of course: my brother, Roger Friedman; Dylan "Clitorious" Ferrero; Cow-

> A happy childhood, I've always believed, is the worst possible preparation for life.
>
> ◆
>
> I've always wanted a lifestyle that didn't require my presence.
>
> ◆
>
> I've come to realize that anyone who uses the word "ambivalent" should never have been a country singer in the first place.

ighter; Bryan "Skycap" Adams; Panama Red; and Arnold "Big Jewford" Shelby, to name just

In 1972 we got our first big break, when Chet Flippo wrote a story about us in *Rolling Stone*. The title of the piece was "Band of Unknowns Fails to Emerge." The following year we did emerge, traveling about the country, irritating many of our fellow Americans. With songs like "They Ain't Makin' Jews Like Jesus Anymore" and "Proud to Be an Asshole From El Paso," we were not destined to be embraced by Mr. and Mrs. Back Porch. In fact, in 1973 the Texas Jewboys received death threats in Nacogdoches, got bomb threats in New York, and required a police escort to escape radical feminists at the University of Buffalo.

> The title of the *Rolling Stone* piece was "Band of Unknowns Fails to Emerge."

We also had an audience with Bob Dylan after a show in Los Angeles (he was barefoot and dressed in white robes), walked on our knuckles after hanging out with Ken Kesey in San Francisco, played a farewell gig for Abbie Hoffman in New York before he went underground (we were cobilled with a video of Abbie's recent vasectomy), and were unceremoniously tossed off the stage by the management of a Dallas nightclub and resurrected the same night at Willie Nelson's house. On June 2, 1973, I had the rare distinction of being introduced by Hank Snow's son, the Reverend Jimmy Snow, as "the first full-blooded Jew ever to appear on the Grand Ole Opry." Through it all the Jewboys believed that the purpose of art is not merely to reflect a culture but to subvert it. We also believed, just as passionately, that some things are too important to be taken seriously.

What happened to the Texas Jewboys? We live in the fine dust of the far horizon, beyond time and geography, where music and dreams play in perfect harmony. Little Jewford and I still occasionally travel the world. He plays keyboards and the most irritating instrument in the musical kingdom, the kazoo. Snakebite Jacobs blows his horn with the New Orleans Nightcrawlers. You can catch him in the Big Easy any Sunday morning. The last time I saw Wichita, who played guitar, mandolin, and fiddle, he was living in his car with his dog, Dwight. Like Mr. Bojangles's dog, Dwight died—from a rattlesnake bite in a trailer park. I would like to find Wichita. Billy Swan wrote "Lover, Please" and "I Can Help" and now lives and makes music in Nashville. My brother, Roger, who originally managed the band, is now a psychologist with three kids and lives in Maryland. Dylan Ferrero, our tour manager who always wore dark shades and a python-skin jacket, now teaches special ed in Comfort and is married to my friend Sage, who has forty tattoos and signs for the deaf.

> I had the rare distinction of being introduced by the Reverend Jimmy Snow as "the first full-blooded Jew ever to appear on the Grand Ole Opry."

The only one who has left us is Jack Slaughter, our road manager. Jack, an expert on forest preservation and endangered animals, was a gentle spirit who always reminded me a bit of Johnny Appleseed. Last year, while jogging on the walkway of the Lamar Street Bridge in Austin, he was killed by an SUV with big tires driven by a teenager. Of all of Jack's accomplishments and after all these years, the obituary in the paper began with "Road manager for the Texas Jewboys." That's not a bad thing, I remember thinking at the time, to have done in your life.

I DON'T

My fairy godmother, Edythe Kruger Friedman, is always telling me I should get married. As the survivor of two happy marriages—the last one to my father—she believes that a man and a woman living together in marital bliss is the only way to find true contentment in life. I believe in a neck without a pain.

Edythe feels so strongly about the importance of marriage and I feel so strongly about the importance of the freedom to wander in the raw poetry of time that often, when I go to her house for breakfast, we get into contentious little arguments on the subject. The debate sometimes becomes so heated that, if you happened to be listening from another room, you might assume that we were married. We are not, of course. I'll never be married. In fact, whenever I'm in Hawaii or Las Vegas or

someplace where I happen to pass by a wedding in progress, I never fail to shout, "Stop before it's too late!"

It's already too late for me. I tell this to Edythe, but she never listens. I explain to her that I'm too old and set in my ways. I'm fifty-eight, though I read at the sixty-year-old level. And just because I'm fifty-eight and I've never been married, I tell her, does not mean I'm gay. It's only one red flag.

But don't you ever want to have a family? Edythe asks, pronouncing the word "family" with a soft reverence, as if it's the most wonderful state of being in the world. Have you ever seen *American Beauty*, I ask her. Families are only acquisition-mergers to create more and more of what there's already more than enough of as it is. It's just a rather narrow, selfish way of creating many little Edythes and many little Kinkys running around taking Ritalin and Prozac, playing video games, saying "awesome," sucking out all the money, energy, and time from your adult life, and growing up with an ever-increasing possibility of becoming the Unabomber. No thanks.

What I don't tell Edythe is that I already have a family. I have four dogs, four women, and four editors. This may seem like an unconventional arrangement to most people, but it does have at least one advantage over a traditional family. I don't have to find schools for them.

> I'm fifty-eight, though I read at the sixty-year-old level.
>
> ◆
>
> Just because I'm fifty-eight and I've never been married . . . does not mean I'm gay. It's only one red flag.

Speaking of school-age kids, another thing I don't tell Edythe is that I'm not really in the market for a fifty-eight-year-old belly dancer. I find myself going out with younger and younger women, most of whom happen to be from Dallas and can't remember where they were when JFK was assassinated, because they weren't born yet. Some of them, in fact, would not be born until several decades later, and they think JFK is an airport, RFK is a stadium, and Martin Luther King is a street running through their town.

"What could you two possibly have to talk about?" my fellow senior citizens often ask. It's true that the only time we ever find common ground is on her futon. She's never heard of Jack

Benny, Humphrey Bogart, or Abbie Hoffman, and she thinks Hitler may have been a punk band in the early eighties. We get along fairly well, because I don't remember much either.

There are two kinds of people in this world, I've always believed. I'm the kind who wants to sleep late and belch loudly and sometimes quite humorously at dinner parties. There are times, undoubtedly, when I feel alone, but I've found that it's always better to feel alone alone than to have that empty, soul-destroying feeling of feeling alone with somebody else. True happiness, I often tell people, must come from within. People don't always like to hear me espouse this great wisdom, but they do seem to prefer it to my belching at dinner parties.

> They think JFK is an airport, RFK is a stadium, and Martin Luther King is a street.

The other kind of person, the polar opposite of myself, is what I like to call the marrying kind. I have three friends who, between them, have been married a dozen times, and I'm betting they're not through yet. Their names are Willie Nelson, Robert Duvall, and Billy Bob Thornton. All three tell me that they still believe in the institution of marriage, especially if it doesn't drive them to the mental institution. I think we're all probably creatures of habit, and the three of them just like being married. Or, possibly, after a failed marriage, the cowboy in them wants to get on that horse again to show he can still ride. A shrink might say they are repetitive neurotics. A shrink might also say that I have a fear of commitment. I would, of course, tell the shrink that I don't have a fear of commitment. I'm just afraid that someday my future ex-wife might not understand me. Then I would tell the shrink I want my money back.

Edythe, however, is oblivious to my protestations and my intransigence. She has a way of approaching the subject from many angles. Don't you ever want to be happy? she sometimes asks. No, I tell her. I don't want to be happy. Happiness is a highly perishable and transitory state, and it doesn't have a balanced export arrangement from one person to another, not to mention that the import tax is too high. Besides, I'm concerned that happiness may have a negative effect on my writing.

Maybe you could write about meeting a nice Jewish girl, my fairy godmother suggests. I've met a lot of nice Jewish girls, I tell her, and they all seem to me to be culturally deprived. They all grew up in this country, yet most of them appear to have never heard the three words that Americans have come to live by.

"I love you?" asks Edythe.

"No," I tell her. "Attention, Wal-Mart shoppers."

Edythe usually continues nattering on until she finally broadsides me with her famous "right person" ploy. Maybe you just haven't found the right person yet, she says. I don't mention it, but I've already found the right person. Unfortunately, she was Miss Fire Ant, 1967. Things went downhill from there, both of us got our feelers hurt, and she wound up putting the bite on me.

> If there's one thing I know about true love, it is that sooner or later it results in a hostage situation.

The conversation usually con-

cludes with Edythe employing what I call the "true love gam-
bit." Don't I believe in true love? Haven't I ever been in true
love? Of course I believe in it, I tell her. I've been in true love
many times. I just try to avoid it as much as possible. For if
there's one thing I know about true love, it is that sooner or
later it results in a hostage situation. Don't get me wrong: I'm
not against marriage. I'm against *my* marriage. Anyway, I'm
rather busy now. It's time to let the dogs in and the editors
out. As for the women, that really isn't necessary. They have
their own inexorable methods of working their way into your
heart.

TEX MY RIDE

———————◆———————

Okay, you just bought a pickup truck and now you think you can pass as a real Texan, right? Think again, hoss. You can't drive off any old car lot and expect your stock truck to be Texas-ready. It takes specific equipment to transform a plain old Amurrrican truck into a real shit kickin', hog haulin' Texas pick-'em-up truck, so before you even think about rolling your raggedy-ass factory vehicle into the Lone Star State, you better take the time to Tex Your Ride! Here's how:

First, get a Ford or Chevy. A Dodge Ram is okay, if you must, but for God's sake don't get anything foreign, I don't care how superior *Consumer Reports* tells you the Toyota Tacoma is. If it ain't American, it ain't Texan, and it never will be. You can put a Diane von Furstenberg silk chiffon dress on a pig, and it's still going to be a pig, you feel me? You can Tex-up a foreign truck but underneath all the accessories, it's still going to be foreign, and therefore it will never be a *real* Texas ride; it will just be another pig wearing a von Furstenberg silk chiffon dress. Trust me on this.

Once you have your American truck, the very first thing you have to do is get a big grill guard, also called a brush guard. This is to protect your front grill from all the debris you'll encounter during the off-road driving you won't be doing. Who would want to bounce around off-road in the mud, especially if you have a four-wheel drive vehicle? If you want to make your penis look bigger, get a winch-ready bull guard, instead of a grill guard. The bull guards are a lot thicker, and they have special mounting features that allow for a winch so that you can pull your imaginary friends out of the mud during your fantasy off-roading.

The same place you get your grill guard will probably also have the little mesh cages for your headlights. Make sure all this aftermarket equipment is flat black. Use your Beretta 9 mm as a swatch—that's the kind of black you want to get. You do have a conceal-carry permit, right?

Next, get some of those daylighters that go on the roof of your Texas ride—you know what I mean, the single row of circular or rectangular lights with the optional yellow smiley face covers that mount on the top of pickup trucks. You need them because you never know when you might feel like doing some "headlighting," shining a row of bright daylighters into a deer's eyes at night, so that they freeze, making it easier for you to shoot them. Headlighting is illegal but so is killing people, which the Texas prison system does with alarming regularity, so don't worry about it. This is Texas!

You've secured grill and headlight protection, a winch, and

auxiliary roof lights. Now you're ready to hoof it to a tire store and swap the factory fagola wheels for some big-ass bogger tires with tread so deep you could hide the neighbor's wetbacks in them. As with anything in Texas, bigger is better. Get the biggest tires and wheels you can afford. While you're at it, go ahead and have the suspension replaced and be sure the truck is lifted *at least* fifteen inches front and rear from the factory ride height.

A Texas truck has to be loud. If you still have any money left, put it into a good exhaust system that will make your pick 'em up roar when you put the pedal to the metal. Don't worry if you can't afford it, though.

A cheaper alternative to getting that aggressive snarl is to punch a hole in your factory exhaust so that it sounds like a leaf blower on steroids when you hit the gas.

Oh, and ignore the nasty looks you get from others when you roar by—they're just jealous. Finally, if you're a rich oil fuck, you'll have enough cash to install a monster top-of-the-line sound system with subwoofers, amplifiers, and a remote level bass control, so you can adjust the settings on your OutKast *Stankonia* CD without having to shift in your seat. Sweet.

Now you have the essentials for any "Tex Your Ride" project. Feel free to scale your Texed-up truck and penetrate our borders with impunity. Once you have secured the basics, you can start procuring the optionals. I suggest a priority be placed on the following:

———•———

- ◆ Faux Navajo blanket seat covers.

- ◆ Black plastic deer whistles you mount on your front bumper to make a high-pitched whistling sound when you drive so that deer don't commit suicide by jumping in front of your vehicle at night—not that it matters, since you have a grill or bull guard to protect your front end and your mufflers are so loud that any living thing within two miles of you has fled the area.

- A window sticker of a cowboy kneeling at the foot of a cross, head bowed, hat in hand.

- A gun rack, which is not as important anymore since the conceal-carry law came into effect.

- A Dallas Cowboys antenna ball in the shape of a helmet.

- Magnetic fake bullet holes, placed down the length of the truck as though your hunting buddy mistook you for a trophy buck.

- A silver running board to give you a boost into the truck cab.

- A hat rack for your Stetson.

———•———

As you can see, options are many, but don't start getting them until you have all the essentials. A true Texas ride can do without the deer whistles, but drive into the state without a grill guard and we give no quarter. You'll get the lethal injection quicker than you can say "Tex My Ride."

WHAT KIND OF TEXAS DRIVER ARE YOU?

———————— ·✦· ————————

Texas drivers generally fall into five different cate-
gories. Take the quiz and see which group fits you
best.

———— ·•· ————

1. You are driving down I-H 10 on a clear fall morning.
Road conditions are excellent and the speed limit is
70. You are most likely to be:

   a. in the fast lane doing 45 mph, oblivious to the traffic jam you are creating behind you.

   b. craning your neck to see over the steering wheel.

   c. alternately tailgating driver "a" and "b" while
   flashing your headlights and honking hysterically.

   d. meditating and trying not to use up any of your

karma points by wishing driver "c" would skid into the grassy median and die in a fiery explosion.

e. throwing your trash out the window.

2. You continue down I-H 10. Your exit is coming up. You will:

a. remain in the fast lane as long as possible, then leisurely mosey across three lanes to take the exit, never noticing the five-car pile-up you leave in your wake.

b. engage your left-turn blinker (even though it's a right turn) and slow your Cadillac down to a fast walk, six miles before your exit comes up. You leave your left turn signal on for the rest of your trip.

c. make three hundred lane changes in five minutes, ending up where you began, in the far left lane. At the last possible moment, you cut diagonally across all three lanes only to slam on your brakes because the guy you ended up behind was rude enough to patiently stay in his lane and safely signal his exit before you ran your rice burner Toyota up his ass.

d. exit, then sprinkle sage out the window and bless the universe for guiding you safely off the highway on your journey to Whole Foods Market.

e. miss the exit, but just exit anyway, driving through guardrails and safety barrels until you get to the access road.

3. You approach a busy intersection as the traffic light is turning yellow. You are roughly twenty yards away. Most likely, you would:

   a. never notice the light, let alone that it has turned yellow. Continue driving 30 mph slower than the traffic around you.
   b. stop as soon as you see the light turn yellow, despite the fact that you are twenty yards from the intersection.
   c. floor it to beat the light and narrowly miss running over the mentally retarded gentleman who is selling roses on the corner at the intersection.
   d. bring your car to a gentle stop, close your eyes, and meditate for world peace.
   e. pop open another beer and see if you can chug the whole can by the time the light turns green.

4. You have just entered a store parking lot. You are most likely to:

   a. park in the pedestrian crosswalk right in front of the store and leave your vehicle idling while you go inside and spend an hour tasting all the free samples. You exit the store without buying a thing.
   b. find a spot you want and wait for the person parked there to return, so you can have it, all the while positioned in the middle of the road so no one can get around you.

   c. circle the lot at least fifty times to get a space as
   close to the store as possible. When none opens up,
   park in the handicapped spot and straddle the
   lines so you take up two spaces.

   d. park two miles from the store and take the bus
   the rest of the way, feeling happy that for the moment you aren't personally contributing to global
   warming.

   e. park, then pee next to your truck in full view of the
   lunch crowd at Luby's.

5. You are driving through a construction zone. Traffic is
moving very slowly. You notice a car on a side street
trying to make a right-hand turn into your lane in
front of you. You will:

   a. do nothing. You are driving even slower than
   everyone else, so the other car has plenty of time to
   make his turn in front of you.

   b. crane your neck to see over the steering wheel,
   then slam on your brakes and panic when you see
   all the traffic.

   c. cut the guy off by pulling up so close to the car in
   front of you that a piece of dental floss couldn't
   even squeeze between your bumpers. Glare at the
   other driver to make sure he knows you hate him.

   d. visualize healing light surrounding the other car
   like a sweet mist as you wave them ahead with a
   smile. When they flip you off, ring your Buddhist
   temple bell and mentally go to your happy place.

e. grab one of your seventy-nine handguns and see if you can reload the whole clip by the time the other driver turns in front of you. Celebrate your new reloading record by popping open another can of beer and draining it in one gulp. Throw the empty can out the window.

———————

Note: Tally the number of As, Bs, Cs, Ds, and Es you marked. Determine which letter you scored the most and match it with the driver style profile below.

Mostly As, you are a *San Antonio Stroller*:

You amble along in a beat-up Frankenstein vehicle (an automobile pieced together with junkyard parts from twenty different cars). Your license plates have been expired for four years because you can't renew them unless you show proof of insurance, which you don't have because you never got a driver's license. You drive 45 mph in the fast lane, oblivious to the traffic jam behind you.

Mostly Bs, you are a *Kerrville Codger*:

You clench the steering wheel so tightly your knuckles are white. Your vision is limited to what you can see through the top of your steering wheel because you can't see over it. Your car is usually a late model Cadillac. You drive a consistent 25 mph whether you're on the freeway or in a parking lot. You frequently mistake your gas pedal for your brake. Luckily, you can't see or hear, so you think other drivers are generally pretty nice.

Mostly Cs, you are a *Houston Rocket*:

You never stop accelerating or slamming on the brakes. You are compelled to always be first, even if it means you have to go 110 mph because the asshole you're trying to pass on the right won't slow down. You weave through traffic impatiently, making no less than thirty lane changes a minute. You tailgate and blink your headlights at the car in front of you to make them get out of your way, even if there is nowhere for them to go. If a driver even thinks about cutting in front of you, you feign sideswiping them to teach the offending driver a lesson. How else will they learn?

Mostly Ds, you are an *Austin Altruistic*:

You drive an environmentally friendly Toyota Prius hybrid car that gets 58.3 miles per gallon. Your bumper is covered with stickers that reflect your benevolent global view (SAVE THE BARTON SPRINGS SALAMANDER being prominent among them). You believe in random acts of kindness, feeding the poor, tree pixies, and being depressed.

Mostly Es, you are a *Bandera Bullet-head*:

You drive a battered pickup truck with a wire coat-hanger antennae, so you can listen to your favorite AM radio talk shows. You wear a cowboy hat that's older than your wife. The floorboard of your vehicle is littered with empty beer cans and cigarette butts. On the front seat of your "hick-up" truck, you have a twelve-gauge shotgun, three high-powered hunting rifles with nightscopes, seventy-nine handguns, and a beer cooler full of armor-piercing bullets.

THE
HUMMINGBIRD
MAN

A wise old man named Slim, who wore a paper Rainbow bread cap, drank warm Jax beer in infinite quantities, listened faithfully to the hapless Houston Astros on the radio, and washed dishes at our family's ranch, once told me something I've never forgotten. He said, "You're born alone and you die alone, so you might as well get used to it." It didn't mean much to me then, but over the years I've come to believe that old Slim might have been on to something.

I live alone now in the lodge, where my late parents once lived, and I'm getting used to it. Being a member of the Orphan Club is not so bad. Sooner or later, fate will pluck us all up by our pretty necks. If you have a family of your own, maybe you won't feel it quite as much. Or maybe you will. I'm married to the wind, and my children are my animals and the books I've written, and I love them all. I don't play favorites. But I miss my mom and dad. In the past fifty years, thousands of kids have known Uncle Tom and Aunt Min. They bought our ranch outside Medina in 1952, named it Echo Hill, and made it into a camp for boys and girls. Echo Hill will be open again this summer, and though the kids will ride horses, swim in the river, and explore the hills, they will not get to meet Uncle Tom and Aunt Min.

> "You're born alone and you die alone, so you might as well get used to it."
> —SLIM

My mother died in May 1985, just a few weeks before camp started, and my father died in August 2002, just a few weeks after camp was over. I can still see my mother at her desk, going over her cluttered clipboard with all the camp rosters and menus. I can see her at the Navajo campfire, at the big hoedown, at the friendship circle under the stars. I can see my dad wearing a pith helmet and waving to the kids in the charter buses. I can see him raising the flag in the morning, slicing the watermelon at picnic suppers, sitting in a lawn chair out in front of the lodge, talking patiently to a kid having problems with his bunkmates. If you saw him sitting quietly there, you'd think he was talking to one of his old friends. Many of those kids became just that.

I don't know how many baby fawns ago it was, how many stray dogs and cats ago, or how many homesick kids ago, but fifty years is a long time in camp years. Yet time, as they say, is the money of love. And Tom and Min put a lot of all those things into Echo Hill. Most of their adult lives were given over to children, daddy longlegs, arrowheads, songs, and stars. They lived in a little green valley surrounded by gentle hills, where the sky was as blue as the river, the river ran pure, the waterfalls sparkled clear in the summer sun, and the campfire embers never really seemed to die. I was just a kid, but looking back, that's the way I remember it.

> Time, as they say, is the money of love.

What I remember most of all are the hummingbirds. It might have been 1953 when my mother hung out the first hummingbird feeder on the front porch of the lodge. The grown-up, outside world liked Ike that year and loved Lucy, and Hank Williams died, as did Ethel and Julius Rosenberg. I believe now that I might have been vaguely aware of these things occurring even back then, but it was those tiny, wondrous rainbows of flying color that really caught my eye. And those first few brave hummingbirds had come thousands of miles, all the way from Mexico and Central America, just to be with us at Echo Hill. Every year the hummers would make this long migration, arriving almost precisely on March 15, the Ides of March. They would leave late in the summer, their departure usually depending upon how much fun they had had at camp.

For those first few years, in the early fifties, the hummingbird population, as well as the number of campers, was fairly sparse, but as the green summers flashed by, more and more kids and hummingbirds came to Echo Hill. The hummingbirds nested every year in the same juniper tree next to the lodge. Decades later, after my mother's death, the tree began to die as well. Yet even when there were only a few green branches left, the hummers continued to make that tree their summer home. Some of the staff thought the tree was an eyesore and more than once offered to cut it down, but Tom wouldn't hear of it. I think he regarded the hummingbirds as little pieces of my mother's soul.

My father and I more or less took over the hummingbird program together in 1985. As time went by, we grew into the job. It was amazing how creatures so tiny could have such a profound influence on your peace of mind and the way you looked at the world. My father, of course, did many other things besides feeding the hummingbirds. I, unfortunately, did not. That was how I gradually came to be known as the Hummingbird Man of Echo Hill.

> I think he regarded the hummingbirds as little pieces of my mother's soul.

Tom and I disagreed, sometimes almost violently, about the feeding methods for these fragile little creatures. He measured exactly four scoops of sugar and two drops of red food coloring into the water for each feeder. I eyeballed the whole process, using much more sugar and blending many weird colors into the mix. Whatever our disagreements over methodology, the hummer population grew. This past summer, it registered more than a hundred birds at "happy hour." Tom confided to me that once, long ago, he mixed a little gin in with the hummers' formula and they seemed to have a particularly lively happy hour. Min was not happy about it, however, and firmly put a stop to this practice.

Now, on bright, cold mornings, I stand in front of the old

lodge, squinting into the brittle Hill Country sunlight, hoping, I suppose, for an impossible glimpse of a hummingbird or of my mother or my father. They've all migrated far away, and the conventional wisdom is that only the hummingbirds are ever coming back. Yet I still see my mother hanging up that first feeder. The juniper tree blew down in a storm two winters ago, but the hummers have found other places to nest. One of them is in my heart.

And I still see my dad sitting under the dead juniper tree, only the tree doesn't seem dead, and neither does he. It takes a big man to sit there with a little hummingbird book, taking the time to talk to a group of small boys. He is telling them that there are more than three hundred species of hummingbird. They are the smallest of all birds, he says, and also the fastest. They're also, he tells the kids, the only birds who can fly backward. The little boys seem very excited about the notion of flying backward. They'd like to try that themselves, they say. So would I.

"See you Monday, Mr. Ronson, and by the way, I've *definitely concluded* that you *don't* have a multiple-personality problem!"

✶ PART II ✶

ROOM WITH A BOO

THE HOUSEGUEST

Yes, those news reports are true. I did spend a night at the White House as a guest of President and Mrs. Bush. It's not true that I slept in the Lincoln Bedroom, but I did visit the place, and I hung out there long enough to bounce on the bed and soak up what residual ambience remained after Steven Spielberg, Barbra Streisand, and half of Hollywood had done their best to suck out some of its soul.

Kinkster, you're probably asking, how in the hell did you get to the White House in the first place? By limo, of course— by special White House limo, blue as the deep blue sea. It picked me up just in the nick of time in front of Washington's posh Willard Hotel, where I'd been waiting with my friend, Jimmie "Ratso" Silman, the little Lebanese boy in my band.

The doormen at the Willard were obviously ignorant of my talents, and the situation was not helped by the fact that Ratso and I were wearing large black cowboy hats and that Ratso, who looks a bit like Saddam Hussein in a jovial mood, kept shouting, "Kinky's goin' to the White House! Kinky's goin' to the White House!"

In the end, of course, Ratso was vindicated, and I was quickly whisked over to a large portico of the White House where many news photographers had gathered to watch the president depart by helicopter for a speech in Virginia. I was escorted inside and deposited at one end of a huge, ornately furnished empty corridor that wasn't empty for long, because the president, accompanied by several aides, soon appeared at the other end, rushing toward me. He gave me a big hug, then hurried for the helicopter, shouting over his shoulder, "I'll be back soon, Kink. Make yourself at home."

In a flash he was gone, and I was standing alone in the White House with my busted valise. Before long, a friendly hostess came up and escorted me down the hallway. "Your room is on the third floor in the family compound," she said. "You're right across the hall from the solarium, where you can smoke your cigars. Hughie used to smoke there."

"Hughie?" I said.

"Hughie Rodham," she said. "Hillary's brother."

Some of the romance of getting to smoke a cigar in the White House is knowing that you're following in the smoke rings of great men. Maybe you're puffing peacefully away in the very chair where Thomas Jefferson once stoked a stogie. Or Teddy Roosevelt, Mark Twain, or Winston Churchill.

Somehow Hughie Rodham wasn't quite the historical predecessor I was hoping for.

After dropping off my stuff, I took a stroll through the solarium and exited a side door onto the balcony. I found a chair, lit a cigar, and looked over the foreboding landscape of the nation's capital. The time and place was not lost upon me. It was December 7, 2001, Pearl Harbor Day, and the whole country was waiting for the other terrorist shoe to drop, and I was sitting on a balcony at the White House, what could well be the prime target of the enemy. I glanced up at the roof and saw two ninja-like figures, dressed entirely in black, creeping along the roof with automatic weapons. "I hope they're ours," I said to the Washington Monument.

> Some of the romance of getting to smoke a cigar in the White House is knowing that you're following in the smoke rings of great men.

"Stand tall," the monument replied.

By the time I got back to my room, a tray of rather coochi-poochi-boomalini hors d'oeuvres had been placed on the table and a beautiful hand-blown Christmas tree ornament in the shape of the White House and signed by President and Mrs. Bush was nestled in gift-wrapping on my bed. As a proud Red Sea pedestrian, I normally don't have a lot of uses for Christmas tree ornaments. I figured I'd either have to hang it or hang myself, and at the moment, I was leaning toward the latter. I hadn't seen a human being in quite a while now, and the somewhat disturbing notion crossed my mind that if the president didn't come back soon, I might have to become an Alexander Haig impersonator and take over the government.

Several hours later my fears were assuaged as I joined the president and a group of about forty family members and friends in the State Dining Room for dinner. I found myself seated at Laura Bush's right. Politically speaking, I'm not sure if I'm to the right of Laura Bush, but she's a woman who definitely has her own ideas. I took a chance and asked her if she'd headline a benefit in Austin for the Utopia Animal Rescue Ranch. I told her that I'd already asked Willie Nelson, who'd said yes and then backed out. Willie will say yes to anything that's more than two weeks away. I mentioned that I'd also approached Lyle Lovett, but that was just before Lyle had been approached by a large, angry bull. "So I'm your third choice," the first lady said thoughtfully. "Okay, I'll do it." Thanks to her, the event was a big financial pleasure.

> As a proud Red Sea pedestrian, I normally don't have a lot of uses for Christmas tree ornaments.
>
> ◆
>
> "So I'm your third choice," the first lady said thoughtfully. "Okay, I'll do it."
>
> ◆
>
> I feel close to the Bush family in the same way that I feel close to the Willie Nelson family and the Charles Manson family.

After dinner, the president asked me to read some of my writing, which I did, working without a microphone, walking around between the tables like a slightly ill mariachi. It was a heady experience for a young cowboy who hadn't actively supported a political candidate since Ralph Yarborough went to Jesus. Friendship, it seems, can sometimes transcend politics. I must admit that now I feel close to the Bush family in the same way that I feel close to the Willie Nelson family and the Charles Manson family. Maybe I'm just a lonely guy looking for a family.

What I remember most vividly about that night was smoking cigars with the president on the Truman Balcony and talking about baseball— specifically, his throwing out the first pitch at the World Series. With the excitement of being on the field at Yankee Stadium and the threat of a terrorist attack, how had he managed to toss a perfect strike, I wanted to know? None of that bothered him, he said. What was on his mind was something that Derek Jeter, the Yankees shortstop, had told him before the game: "Whatever you do, don't bounce the ball on the way to the plate. They don't care who you are—they'll boo you."

> **"Whatever you do, don't bounce the ball on the way to the plate. They don't care who you are—they'll boo you."**
> —DEREK JETER

MAD COWBOY
DISEASE

In *The Innocents Abroad,* Mark Twain observed, "They spell it 'Vinci' and pronounce it 'Vinchy'; foreigners always spell better than they pronounce." Twain didn't mention it, but they also spell better than they smell. All in all, very little seems to have changed since his time. There's nothing like a trip across the old herring pond to make you glad that you live in the good ol' USA.

I knew that early March wasn't the best time to be a cowboy in Europe, yet I felt I had to honor a commitment I'd made to address an event in London with an unfortunate title: "Murder at Jewish Book Week." Everyone told me it was sheer idiocy to travel overseas with the triple threats of war, terror, and customs inspectors taking away my Cuban cigars. Yet, strangely, it wasn't courage that compelled me to go. It was simply that I was afraid at that late date to tell the lady I was canceling.

The flight was nine and a half hours long. It seemed as if almost every passenger besides myself was dressed in some form or other of Middle Eastern garb. One young man who spoke English was wearing a Muslim prayer cap and robe over a University of Texas sweatshirt. He told me there was really nothing to be concerned about. "You have gangsta chic," he explained. "We have terrorist chic." I found his calm analysis oddly comforting.

> **There's nothing like a trip across the old herring pond to make you glad that you live in the good ol' USA.**

I was totally jet-lagged when I arrived at London's Gatwick Airport at 6:55 in the morning. My ride into town was arranged by Robert MacNeil of the old *MacNeil/Lehrer NewsHour*. The day before, I'd been filming a PBS show with Robert in Bandera and had warned him about crossing the busy streets of the little cowboy town. "It'd seem quite ridiculous," I'd told him, "for a cosmopolitan figure like yourself to get run over in Bandera." MacNeil just said that he didn't want the headline to read, KINKY FRIEDMAN SEES MAN KILLED.

As I walked the cobbled streets, visited pubs and restaurants, played songs, and did interviews with the BBC, the subject of President Bush and Iraq popped up often, sometimes acrimoniously. I found myself defending my president, my country, and my cowboy hat. Soon I was going on the preemptive attack myself, calling every mild-mannered Brit who engaged me in conversation a "crumpet-chomping, Neville

"I'M SAYIN' YOU'RE ALL YELLA!"

Chamberlain, surrender monkey." After a while, I realized the futility of this approach and merely told people that I was from a mental hospital and was going to kill them.

Bright and early the next morning, my journalist friend Ned Temko took me on a quest for Cuban cigars, which are legal in London, if expensive. Everything is legal in London, if expensive. Phil the Tobacconist mentioned that Fidel Castro personally supplies Cuban cigars to Saddam Hussein. "I wouldn't write about that," said Ned. "George W. might nuke Fidel." As the three of us entered the walk-in humidor, Ned revealed that he'd once covered Iraq for the *Christian Science*

Monitor in the late seventies. "Saddam's a thug with an excellent tailor," Ned said.

"I know his tailor," Phil said. "He's right down the street, in Savile Row."

Meeting Saddam's tailor is almost as special as meeting Gandhi's barber, but I felt I had to try. Ned, my Virgil of Savile Row, led us down the

> **"Saddam's a thug with an excellent tailor."**
> —NED TEMKO

winding streets to a discreet-looking row of shops where tweeds were being measured for dukes and dictators behind closed shutters. Maybe it was the cowboy hat and high rodeo drag that prevented entry, or maybe it was simply the lack of an appointment, but at the designated address, no one came to the door. My outfit did get an enthusiastic response, however, from a group of city workers repairing the street nearby. They stopped what they were doing and sang cheerfully together, "I'm a rhinestone cowboy!"

"Since we didn't see Saddam's tailor," Ned said, "why don't we try to meet Tony Blair?"

"Jesus," I said.

"That's what the Yanks may think," said Ned. "Over here, they're about to crucify him."

Twenty minutes later, we were standing next to a Wimbledon-style grass tennis court hidden in the heart of London. "We may be in luck," said Ned. "There's Mike Levy." Levy, Ned explained, was a former record producer who'd given the world early-seventies glam rocker Alvin Stardust. "What's he done for us lately?" I wanted to know.

"He's Tony Blair's tennis partner," he said.

Levy was in a hurry, and it didn't seem likely that Blair had played tennis that morning. Still, ever the innocent American, I stepped forward as Levy was climbing into his roadster.

"Anything you'd like to say about Tony Blair?" I asked.

"Yes," Levy said. "He needs to work on his backhand."

On my last night in London, I walked through the fog until I came to the most famous address in the world, 221B Baker Street. On the door was a small bronze plaque that read, VISITORS FOR MR. SHERLOCK HOLMES OR DOCTOR WATSON PLEASE RING THE BELL. I rang the bell, walked up one flight of seventeen steps, and suddenly I was standing in Sherlock Holmes's living room. There was a cheery fire in the fireplace. Holmes's violin stood poignantly nearby, along with the old Persian slipper where he kept his Turkish tobacco. And in the room were Japanese, Russians, Africans, people from seemingly every nation on earth, all bound together by a common, passionate belief that Sherlock Holmes was real. It was, I thought, a perfect United Nations.

> "Ever seen a real cowboy before?" I asked. "No," she said. "But I've seen a cow."

The next morning I was waiting in line at the airport to board a plane back to the States. Behind me was a proper British couple with a shy little girl clutching her teddy bear and staring intently at my hat. "Ever seen a real cowboy before?" I asked.

"No," she said. "But I've seen a cow."

YOU'RE A HARDCORE TEXAN IF . . .

- You've ever eaten a four-pound steak in under one hour in one sitting at a restaurant in Amarillo.

- You have a toilet seat cover in the shape of an armadillo.

- Your children are named Austin, Houston, Dallas, Travis, and Maria.

- Your dog can keep his balance while perched atop a toolbox in the back of a pickup truck going 70 mph in a hailstorm.

- Your biggest culinary decision is barbecue sauce or salsa.

- When you see red, white, and blue you think of the Lone Star flag before you think of Old Glory.

- Every morning at school your child recites the Texas Pledge after the Pledge of Allegiance (followed by a moment of silence).

- You have ever gone to your pet's vet for your own illnesses and injuries.

- You lose all ability to drive, walk, or work when you see a single snowflake.

- You think turquoise blue is a stupid color for a pack of cigarettes.

- You have every episode of *The Best of Bassmasters Tournament* on DVD.

- You have to drive to your roadside mailbox. Extra hardcore if it's so far you have to pack a lunch.

- You have ever expressed disappointment that the grocery store was out of potted meat.

- You cry every time you get to the part where the Alamo fell to Santa Anna's army.

- You cheer every time you get to the part where the Texans yelled, "Remember the Alamo," during the victorious Battle of San Jacinto.

- You know how to correctly pronounce "San Jacinto" (san-ha-SIN-toe).

TEXAS FIRSTS

- The nation's first rodeo competition was held in Pecos, Texas, in 1883.

- The Fort Worth Zoo was the first in the nation to create a replica of a rain forest.

- The first powered airplane in the world was flown in Texas nearly forty years before the Wright Brothers' famous flight in 1903. Jacob Brodbeck, the inventor-pilot, flew the coil-spring powered airplane in 1865, reportedly reaching treetop heights before crashing into a chicken roost.

- Highland Park Village Shopping Center in Dallas, Texas, developed in 1931, holds the distinction of being the first shopping mall in America.

- *Wings*, the first movie to win an Academy Award for Best Picture, was shot in and around San Antonio.

- The first sauropod tracks discovered in the world were found at Dinosaur Valley State Park near Glen Rose, Texas.

- The first domed-roof arena built in the United States was the Will Rogers Coliseum, built in Fort Worth in 1936.

- The first word spoken from the moon on July 20, 1969, was "Houston."

- Miriam A. "Ma" Ferguson was the second woman to serve as governor in the United States, but because of the date of elections in Texas, she was technically the first woman elected to that office. She served from 1925 to 1927 and again from 1933 to 1935.

- The first person to fly around the world alone was Texan Wiley Post, of Grand Saline. He left Floyd Bennett Field, New York City, July 15, 1933, and returned seven days, eighteen hours, forty-nine and a half minutes later. He was also the first person to fly around the world twice.

- The nation's first convenience stores, the vast 7-Eleven chain, now in eighteen countries, started in Dallas in 1922.

- In 1938, also in Dallas, Hillcrest State Bank opened the first drive-up bank window.

ARDOR IN THE COURT

At a recent book signing of mine at Murder by the Book, in Houston, I was pleased to see the legendary defense lawyer Racehorse Haynes making his way through the crowd. Little Jewford, the last surviving member of the Texas Jewboys, had just introduced me as "the next governor of the great state of Texas," and I had assured him that I would keep him on the short list for first lady. It was at that point that Racehorse came up to the microphone and, in true lawyerly fashion, managed to endorse my candidacy without actually endorsing my candidacy. He said his real views on the Kinkster were "privileged and must remain privileged." Then he introduced his wife, Naomi, as "the widow Haynes." I was commenting on what an honor it would be to have Racehorse in a Friedman administration, working pro bono to fix

the broken criminal justice system, when David Berg, a pro-
tégé of Racehorse and a brilliant lawyer in his own right, suddenly leaped from his seat. "The words 'Racehorse' and 'pro
bono,' " he shouted, "are never used in the same sentence!"

Why are so many legal eagles—or buzzards, as the case may be—big fans of my books? Do they see me as the thinking man's John Grisham? How the hell should I know? All I'm sure of is that quite often at my book signings, a long line of lawyers will surreptitiously snake its way past the little old ladies with their aluminum Jerry Jeff Walkers. Whenever this happens, I find the lawyers in con-tempt of bookstore and send them to the back of the room. Still, so many of them turn up at these events that I've almost had to stan-dardize my book inscriptions to them. While they are perverse enough to like "From one left-handed Jewish homosexual to another," they appear to appreciate more deeply something that acknowledges their oft-maligned profession. Thusly, to borrow a bit of legalese, two favored inscriptions for lawyers have evolved. The first is, "Where there's a will, there's a lawyer." The second is, "May all your juries be well hung."

There is, however, a small but growing pantheon of lawyers I have come to know and, yes, admire—from Jim Schropp, a corporate attorney in Washington, D.C., who has spent the

> Racehorse came up to the microphone and, in true lawyerly fashion, managed to endorse my candidacy without actually endorsing my candidacy.
>
> ◆
>
> "The words 'Race-horse' and 'pro bono,' " he shouted, "are never used in the same sentence!"
> —DAVID BERG

past ten years campaigning vigorously to get Max Soffar off death row, to David Epstein, a Southern Methodist University law school professor, who routinely includes a random question about the Kinkster each year in his national bar review courses. One name on this list has always shone brightly: the aforementioned Racehorse Haynes. If he hadn't owned a yacht, Racehorse would be my candidate to be the Atticus Finch of Texas. In past years, in fact, I sailed with him on said yacht, the *Integrity*. "For those," insists Racehorse, "who say I haven't any."

Racehorse, indeed, is one of the most successful and most colorful silver-tongued devils to grace Texas since God made trial lawyers. When Racehorse was growing up, his Houston family was so poor that, in Moses-like fashion, they had to

leave him in the bulrushes near San Antonio, where his
granny—who was just a hair over four feet tall—taught him
everything he needed to know while drinking a pint of gin
every day. Just to be clear: she was the one drinking. When it
came time to attend elementary
school, Racehorse filled out all the
forms himself and bypassed the first
and second grades. In case you're
wondering, his real name is Richard,
which also happens to be the Kinkster's real name. Possibly
because of Richard Nixon, we grasped at any nicknames we
could get. He got his nickname from a disgruntled junior high
school football coach after little Richard failed to break the
line of scrimmage on two consecutive plays and galloped for
the sidelines. "Goddamn," said the coach sarcastically. "What
do you think you are—a racehorse?"

> **Where there's a will,
> there's a lawyer.**

It would not be possible in this column to do justice to
Racehorse's many victorious battles in the courtroom. "I don't
get people off," he once told me. "The jury acquits them." One
of the people the jury acquitted was T. Cullen Davis, the rich-
est man—by 1976 standards—ever brought to trial on a murder charge. Davis allegedly shot and wounded his wife,
Priscilla, and croaked his stepdaughter and Priscilla's lover
with a .38 in his six-million-dollar mansion on 181 acres near
little old downtown Fort Worth. At the time, Davis claimed to
have been Sirhan Sirhan, party of one, by himself in a movie
theater watching *The Bad News Bears*.

Another famous client of Racehorse was Dr. John Hill, who
allegedly fed his wife an éclair laced with E. coli bacteria.

Toxic shock syndrome was undiagnosed in those days, but experts now agree that Racehorse was once again on the right side of the scales of justice. Then there was the infamous Kerr-

ville "slave ranch" trial, involving drifters who were kidnapped, tortured with a cattle prod, and in at least one instance, killed. Racehorse put on quite a show for the local Kerrverts in front of the courthouse one afternoon. Ever

> **"I don't get people off. The jury acquits them."**
> —RACEHORSE HAYNES

the dedicated defender, he shocked himself repeatedly with an electric cattle prod. "It hurt," he says, "but it wasn't lethal."

In dealing with his famous and not-so-famous clients, there is one rule Racehorse holds inviolable: he almost never allows the defendant to say anything in court. He learned this lesson from a personal experience as a young lawyer. "I believed my guy was innocent, and apparently the jury agreed,"

Another outburst like that and I'll have this courtroom cleared.

says Racehorse. "So when the bailiff handed the verdict to the judge, and the judge declared, 'Not guilty,' I shook hands with my guy and told him he could thank the jury if he wished. So he stands up, and he says to the jury, 'Thank you. I'll never do it again.' "

Racehorse has become every year's model for what a successful trial lawyer should be. He is part Clarence Darrow, part Perry Mason, and part, well, Racehorse Haynes. Yet despite the fact that he has a mansion in River Oaks, sailed until recently on the yacht, and owned a large former slave ranch in the Hill Country (payment for rebuffing those drifters), his lucrative and high-profile triumphs are not what motivate him. That distinction belongs to the case he can't forget, one in the early fifties that earned him no publicity and no fee. In what Racehorse felt was a frame-up, a black man was charged with stealing construction materials. When the jury rendered a verdict of not guilty, the defendant, accompanied by his six little children and his 250-pound wife, began screaming with joy and rushed to hug the young lawyer.

Racehorse went to a party that night at a company shack on the poor side of town. The hors d'oeuvres consisted of leftover barbecue and Coca-Cola. The man was there with his wife, all the kids, and the old grandma. The place was appropriately decorated. The kids had taken their crayons and written on the walls, "God Bless You, Mr. Racehorse."

CASE OPEN

I've seen *Cool Hand Luke* and *The Green Mile*. I like Steve Earle, but I'm not a prison reform activist. I'd never interviewed anyone on death row until the middle of January, when I picked up a telephone and looked through the clear plastic divider at the haunting reflection of my own humanity in the eyes of Max Soffar. Max doesn't have a lot of time and neither do I, so I'll try to keep it brief and to the point. "I'm not a murderer," he told me. "I want people to know that I'm not a murderer. That means more to me than anything. It means more to me than freedom."

Somewhere along the line, Max's life fell between the cracks. A sixth-grade dropout whose IQ tests peg him as borderline mentally retarded, he grew up in Houston, where he was a petty burglar, an idiot-savant car thief, and a low-level if highly imaginative police snitch. He spent four years, he says, "in the nuthouse in Austin," where he remembers the guards putting on human cockfights. They would lock two eleven-year-old boys in a cell, egg them on, and bet on which one would be able to walk out. Max ran away, and it's been pretty much downhill from there.

> "I want people to know that I'm not a murderer. That means more to me than anything. It means more to me than freedom."
>
> —MAX SOFFAR

For the past twenty-three years, since confessing to a cold-blooded triple murder at a Houston bowling alley, Max has been at his final station on the way, the Polunsky Unit, in Livingston. He long ago recanted that confession, and many people, including a number of Houston-area law enforcement officers, think he didn't commit the crime. They say he told the cops what they wanted to hear after three days of interrogation without a lawyer present. At the very least, they say, Max's case is an example of everything that's wrong with the system. In the words of my friend Steve Rambam, who is Max's pro bono private investigator, "I'm not anti–death penalty; I'm just anti-the-wrong-guy-getting-executed." Another observer troubled by Max's case is Fifth Circuit Court of Appeals judge Harold R. DeMoss Jr., who, after hearing Max's last appeal, wrote in the 2002 record, "I have lain awake nights agonizing over the enigmas, contradictions, and ambiguities."

Chief among these Kafkaesque elements is the fact that Max's state-appointed attorney was the late Joe Cannon, who

CALLAHAN

was infamous for sometimes sleeping through his clients' capital murder trials. Cannon managed to stay awake for Max's, but he did not bother to interview the one witness who might have cleared him. There are, incidentally, ten men on death row who were clients of Cannon.

Then there's the evidence—or the total lack of it. Jim Schropp, a Washington, D.C., lawyer, who has been handling Max's case for more than ten years, also on a pro bono basis, says it seemed cut-and-dried when he initially reviewed the file. "But the more we looked into it," he told me recently, "the facts and the confession didn't match up." Schropp discovered that there was no physical evidence linking Max to the crime, no eyewitnesses who placed him at the scene or saw him do it, two police lineups in which Max was not fingered, and missing polygraphs. If the facts had been before them, Schropp says, no jurors would have believed that the prosecution's case had eliminated all reasonable doubt. "When you peel away the layers of the onion," he says, "you find a rotten core."

> "I'm not anti–death penalty; I'm just anti-the-wrong-guy-getting-executed."
> —STEVE RAMBAM
>
> ◆
>
> There are, incidentally, ten men on death row who were clients of Joe Cannon.

Okay, so what about the confession? Rambam says that when Max was arrested on August 5, 1980, for speeding on a stolen motorcycle, it was the third or fourth time he'd been caught for various offenses, and he thought he could deal his way out again, as he'd done before. The bowling alley murders had been highly publicized, and Max had seen the police sketch of the perpetrator, who he thought resembled a friend and sometime running buddy. Max and the friend were on the outs—they'd agreed to rob their parents' houses, but after they robbed Max's parents' house, the friend reneged—so to get revenge and to help his own case in the process, Max volunteered that he knew something about the murders. Unfortunately, in his attempt to implicate his friend, he placed himself at the scene, and before long he became a target of the investigation himself. "The cops spoon-fed Max information, and he gave them what they wanted," Rambam says. "He was a confession machine. If he thought it would have helped him with the police, he would have confessed to kidnapping the Lindbergh baby."

The trouble is, Max's confession—actually, he made three different confessions—contained conflicting information. First, he claimed to be outside the bowling alley when the murders took place and that he only heard the shots. Then he said he was inside and saw it all go down. Then he said his friend shot two people and threw him the gun, whereupon he shot the other two; it was like a scene in an old western. The written record of Max's confession states there were two gunmen, himself and his friend. The only surviving victim, the witness Joe Cannon didn't bother to interview, says there was only one. Max also told the cops that he and his friend had killed some people and buried them in a field. The cops used methane probes and search dogs and found nothing. He claimed that they had robbed several convenience stores, which turned out never to have been robbed. Best of all, when the cops told him that the bowling alley had been burglarized the night before the murders, Max confessed to that crime as well. What he didn't know was that the burglars had already been arrested. "We won't be needing that confession," the homicide detective reportedly told him. After signing the murder confession, Max asked the officers, "Can I go home now?"

> "He was a confession machine. If he thought it would have helped him with the police, he would have confessed to kidnapping the Lindbergh baby."
> —STEVE RAMBAM

You may be wondering, What about the friend? He was arrested solely on the basis of Max's confession but was released because there was no evidence. The same "evidence" was later considered good enough to put Max on death row. Nonetheless, at Max's trial, the prosecutor told the jury the police knew that the friend was involved and that they planned to hunt him down once Max was dealt with. But it never happened. For the past twenty-three years, the friend— who is the son of a Houston cop—has been living free as a bird, currently in Mississippi, with the long arm of the Texas law never once reaching out to touch him. Why? Good question. "It wasn't hard to run him down and pay him a visit," Rambam says. "I found his name in the phone book."

Why would someone confess to a crime he didn't commit? A cry for help? A death wish? Perhaps it has to do with what the poet Kenneth Patchen once wrote: "There are so many little dyings, it doesn't matter which of them is death."

As my interview with Max was ending, he placed his hand against the glass. I did likewise. He said he would like for me to be there with him at the execution if it happens. I hesitated. "You've come this far," he said. "Why go halfway?"

I promised him I would be there. It's a promise I would dearly love not to have to keep.

TEXAS PRISON SLANG

Ace: A drag from a cigarette. "Hook me up with an ace, bro."

Aggie: A long-handled hoe used by inmate work squads in the field. In Texas, a group of field workers form Hoe squads, and the squads are numbered in sequence (one-hoe, two-hoe, etc.).

All day: Serving a life sentence. "That guy's doing all day for robbing that liquor store."

All up in my grill: To aggressively get in someone's face. "I don't know why that C.O.'s all up in my grill lately."

Bale: Loose-leafed tobacco purchased at the canteen.

Bammer/Bama: 1) Cheap, low quality brown leaf marijuana. 2) Something or someone who is not good. "Slim's such a bammer!"

Big bitch: Convicted under the habitual criminal act which carries a mandatory life sentence. *See also* Little bitch.

Big jab: Lethal injection. Also, "stainless steel ride," "doctorate in applied chemistry," or the "needle."

Bonaroo: Your best clothes. "Check you out in your bonaroos!"

Bone: Cigarette.

Boneyard: Family (conjugal) visiting area.

Bootleg: Something that is a cheap imitation or low quality. "I don't want your old bootleg shoes!"

Boss: Considered an acceptable "sir" name for an officer. Prisoners claim it stands for "sorry son of a bitch" spelled backward.

Bought guards: C.O.s who do "favors" for inmates for payment. Not all guards are crooked; many correction officers are honest, hard-working men and women with high standards and respect for themselves and their jobs. Others, however, are opportunists who take advantage of their positions and give a bad reputation to those who would never even consider such highly illegal activities. That being said, bought guards are often paid off by gangs or family members in the free world, so that their homeboys on the inside can take control of the contraband, which the bought guards usually smuggle in, or receive extra favors like better food or preferred units and cells. Bought guards will also pass messages for inmates who live on different sides of the prison, or will pass messages to and from cohorts on the streets. They also set up opportunities for inmate-on-inmate violence, like when they "accidentally" leave cell doors unlocked at night or "mistakenly" put a gang member in the same area with rival gang members and look away when the lone victim is shanked or beaten to a pulp.

Bowling alley: Units that have a long and wide cement walkway. Prisoners walk along the yellow lines on the side of the walkway, while officers and staff walk on the inside.

Box: Segregation, or "the hole." "He got a whole month of box time for gassing that hack."

Brick: A carton of cigarettes.

Brown-eyed girl: Tobacco.

Buck horn: Hand-rolled cigarette.

Bull dagging: Lesbian activities between women; taking a homosexual partner. A "Bull Dagger" is a butch lesbian. *See* Dagging.

Bullet: One-year prison sentence. "They gave me a bullet."

Bumpin ya gums: Talking too much.

Cat-J/J-Cat: A mentally ill prisoner.

Cat nap: A short sentence.

Catch a square: To get ready to fight. "Y'all better catch a square, bitch."

Catch dog: An aggressive corrections officer who is charged with prisoner "discipline"; the discipline is usually meted out while the prisoner is handcuffed and shackled to ensure he doesn't fight back.

Cell gangster: A prisoner who acts tough when he's locked safely in his cell but is meek and quiet when outside his cell. Also known as a "cell warrior" or "cell soldier."

Cellie: Cellmate.

Chain; Chainin': Used when a prisoner is transferred to another unit or arrives and departs on the bus. "Billy went out on the chain last night."

Chalking: To create a distraction while another prisoner is breaking a rule. "Yo, look at that nigga Wolf chalkin'!"

Checking: A fight used to test a new arrival to see whether he will stand up for himself or if he's a punk. *See* Hoe check.

Cho-mo: Child molester.

Chronic: Potent, green, high quality marijuana. "When I was in the world, I only smoked chronic, I never touched this bammer shit I have to smoke in here."

Click: 1) A group of prisoners who look out for each other: a clique. "My click got my back, I ain't worried." 2) When two or more prisoners attack another prisoner. "Skeeter got clicked on the yard yesterday."

Clipper pass: A special shaving pass that allows prisoners with medical conditions to shave only once a week or to wear short beards.

C.O.: Correctional officer. *See also* Boss.

Code 21: Masturbation (from the Texas Department of Corrections offense code).

Commissary; Canteen: Money for buying stamps, deodorant, shampoo, soap, cigarettes, and other items. Also refers to the place to buy it.

Convict: A prisoner who honors the unwritten prison code and who has pride, integrity, and respect. His word is always good and he will never rat you out, even if he hates you. An inmate is the opposite of a convict.

Convict boss: A prisoner given authority in a prison system.

Copping deuces: To say one thing and do another; to change one's mind, pissing others off. "That asshole told me he was gonna score for me, but he coppin' deuces."

Corner: Whom a prisoner hangs out with. Example: "You need to watch out messing with Mario—he got a strong corner backing him."

Count: The institutional count, repeated at different times in the day. Everything stops while prison staff counts heads to make sure no one is missing.

Crate: Another term for a carton of cigarettes.

Crimey: Best friend or codefendant.

Cut that knot: Beat up on a prisoner.

Daddy: A dominant prisoner who protects or uses a weaker prisoner.

Dagging: Trading out for sodomy.

Debrief: A prisoner who wants to officially declare that he is no longer in a gang must "debrief," or give up all information about his gang's members and activities. He will have to name names and detail illegal activities the gang is involved in. He also has to pass a polygraph test about all information he gives. This is the only way a prisoner can officially get rid of his "gang jacket," a gang member label in his central file, and be released from segregation, where prisoners often remain alone in their cell for up to twenty-three hours per day. Once he's given up the goods on his former homeboys he is labeled a snitch, which is the most hated man in an environment full of hate. In essence, debriefing is a lose-lose proposition, because a snitch label follows a man everywhere and he will be despised no matter where he is transferred. Prisoners who are wrongfully identified as gang members, whether by accident or by a vengeful C.O., are stuck, because they have no inside information on a gang they don't belong to and it's near impossible to prove otherwise.

Deck: Pack of cigarettes. *See also* Square.

Dirt nap: To die.

Dog; Dawg: Homeboy or friend. "You my dawg!"

Down: 1) To be faithful to a friend or group; to be loyal enough to fight to the end for someone. "I'm down with you, dawg." 2) Concur or agree with. "Don't sweat it, man, I'm down with whatever you decide."

Elbow (L-Bow): Life sentence.

EME: The Mexican Mafia, a powerful prison gang. *Eme* is Spanish for the letter "m."

Escape dust: Fog.

Featherwood: A peckerwood's woman.

Feel me: To understand what someone means. "Y'all better move on or I'll move y'all on, you feel me?"

Fish: A new prisoner.

Flat wig: To slam someone down hard onto the floor. Also called "flat weed."

Ford: "Found On Run Dead." The myth goes that once upon a time at a long-forgotten prison, a doctor named "Ford" was so bad that any prisoner he treated either got worse or died. "Ford" evolved to mean any inept or uncaring prison doctor.

Free world: The outside.

Free world cash: Legal tender; cash currency. Prisoners are not allowed to have any paper money or coins on the inside but most do, hiding it in their cells or on their person. Denominations are usually tens and twenties and are used to pay for drugs or tobacco. For related, *see also* Stamps.

Free world folks: A prisoner's family or friends on the outside who can do all kinds of things to support him while he's doing time, like send money for his canteen account, arrange and/or carry out "business," bring in contraband, or simply love him and wait for the day he returns back to the free world. Free world folks are essential to an inmate.

Galboy: A person who plays a female role in a homosexual relationship.

Gassing: Throwing a cocktail of body fluids at an officer from a cell. Also called "dashing."

Gate money: The small amount of money a prisoner is given when he's released.

General population/Gen-Pop/Pop/G.P.: The part of prison where prisoners can mingle with other prisoners.

Gladiator fight: Fights set up by guards or inmates for entertainment. A gladiator school is a facility where these kinds of fights are common.

Grilling: When someone bares their teeth at you, showing how many gold teeth they have or just showing their teeth. This is usually considered an invitation to fight. "Did you see J. T. grilling on me just now?"

Handle up on your business: To fight someone.

High-five: H.I.V.

Hit in the neck/He's hit: Despondent, resigned, having no hope. "Oh, hell! Tony just heard his mom died . . . he's hit now."

Hoe check: Ganging up on a prisoner to see if he will fight back and defend himself. Also known as "check" or "checking."

Hog: A prisoner who will fight back to defend himself, therefore not an easy target.

Homes: 1) A greeting to another person. "Hey, homes!" 2) A prisoner's cell. "Yo, I'll see y'all later, I'm going home."

Hooped: Hiding contraband in the rectum. "He gets all his money by hooping weed."

Hot rail: When prisoners make a human barrier around a fellow inmate so he can grope or have sex with his girlfriend/wife on visitor's day without the C.O.'s noticing.

In the car: To belong to a close-knit circle of friends who will stay loyal to one another to the death.

In the hat: Targeted for death. Term is said to originate from "back in the day." Convicts who wanted to kill someone like a snitch, would tear five or six strips of paper. Only one paper would have the victim's name on it and each convict would draw a piece of paper from a hat or cap. If a con got the paper with the name on it, he had to kill the victim. No one was to acknowledge what he drew, so in the end, after the deed was done, only the killer and the victim would know who actually carried out the hit.

Inmate: A prisoner who does not honor the values of the prison world. An inmate is usually a young, reckless, inexperienced person who eventually either gets "schooled" by older prisoners or killed by other inmates.

Jacket: A prisoner's central file that follows him wherever he goes in the system. If the prisoner is an informer, his file is labeled as such and he is said to have a "rat jacket." If he is a gang member, he is said to have a "gang jacket."

Joes: Cigarettes.

Keister: To hide contraband in the rectum.

Keister bunny: Someone who hides contraband in the rectum. Also called a "mule."

Kill: To masturbate. "Every single night my cellie kill to that picture of his woman and I can't get no sleep!"

Kite: Notes or letters passed to a prisoner. "My old high school buddy just got transferred here—I need to shoot him a kite."

K-9: Corrections officer (canine).

Krunk: Exciting, giddy, wild; unfettered fun. "My homeboys threw me a party on my last night in the free world and it was straight up krunk!"

Lag: A convict; the opposite of "lop."

Little bitch: A sentence of fifty or more years. *See also* Big bitch.

Lop: A prisoner who is looked upon as stupid or unworthy; an "inmate." The opposite of "lag."

Mad dawg/Mad dog: To give someone a long and lingering look from head to toe. "You mad dawging me, bitch? I'll cap your ass!"

May tag: 1) Passive person in a homosexual relationship. 2) An inmate who is forced to (or paid to) wash clothes for another.

On the one: Honest. Taken from George Washington on the one-dollar bill. "You know I'll pay you back, man, I'm on the one!"

Onion: A girl with a large ass. "Flip's bitch got a fine onion."

Parlayin': Relaxing and kicking back. "It's visitor's day so I guess Mike's down there parlayin' with his woman."

Parole dust: Fog.

Partner; Pahtna: (pronounced "pawt-na") A friend, someone who is loyal to you. "He's cool, he's my partner."

Passenger: A friend, someone who is "in the car."

Pearl handle: A commercial cigarette.

Pecker palace: A place for conjugal visits. *See also* Trailer privileges.

Peckerwood: A white prisoner. Originally used in disdain, but it has evolved to describe a white who is down with his race.

Peels: The orange jumpsuit worn in some jails and prisons.

Pencil whipped: To be given a discipline notice by a C.O.

Perpetratin': To act like something you're not. "That fish walk up in here perpetratin' like that, it's time for a hoe check."

Phone: A toilet can be emptied of water and used to talk to other prisoners while in segregation or during lockdown. "Yo, Freddie! Get on the phone, man, I got to tell you something!"

Pound: A compound or yard a prisoner belongs to. "Things are getting crazy on my pound lately."

Pound it: Tapping your fist on your friend's fist and vice versa. "Pound it, homes."

Prize of the poor: The death penalty.

Pruno: Homemade alcohol, the quintessential prison beverage of choice. While there are different methods to make pruno, one way is to take a case of fruit cocktail and open the cans, drain off some of the juice, and add yeast and sugar stolen from the kitchen. The sugared-up fruit cocktails are then hidden near a heat source, like the big ovens used to cook mess hall food (the heat activates the yeast and thus increases the proof). The mixture is left to ferment for about a week or so and is then either consumed or used as currency inside the unit.

Put your pen to the wind: Uttered by a prisoner to tell a C.O. to go ahead and write a disciplinary report.

Road dogs: Prisoners who walk or work out together on the exercise yard. Road dogs are also loyal friends who will stick together to the end, on the inside or on the outside.

Road kill: Tobacco that is extracted from discarded cigarette butts. Prisoners assigned to the road cleanup crews gather discarded cigarette butts from the side of the road and take them back to their cell where the tobacco is carefully harvested and rerolled.

Scrilla/Scrill: Money.

Shot caller: A high-ranking prisoner on the yards who directs action/discipline. If a prisoner wants to kill or injure another prisoner, he better make sure he gets the shot caller's permission first just in case the intended victim owes the shot caller a debt (because the guy who does the unsanctioned hit will end up footing his victim's bill). "I talked to the shot caller and he gave me the okay to take that wetback out."

Six: To watch someone's back. "My road dog got my six."

Skid bid: Short sentence.

Spider monkey: Someone doing hard time to the point where he's climbing the walls.

Split your wig: A quick punch to the head.

Square: Cigarette.

Stamps: The most valuable currency circulated in prison. On the inside, you can buy anything for postal stamps: drugs, tobacco, sex, anything. Knowing this, most states limit the number of stamps an inmate may have in his possession at any given time to try to discourage this popular payment technique, but prisoners just work around this rule by having their homies hold their extra stamps for them until they need something on the black market. The convict then simply rounds up all his stamps from his various friends and pays for his goods. He will then pay off his holder friends with some of the black market goods.

Stole: To get sucker punched. "That peckerwood really stole you, man."

Suit casing: Carrying drugs or other contraband in the rectum.

Swoll/Swole: Angry. "He got all swoll at me." Also means very muscular.

Teardrop: Ten-year sentence.

Teardrop tattoo: A teardrop shaped tattoo placed near the corner of the eye. It can represent the bearer's prison time or in remembrance of a friend killed while the bearer was in prison.

Taking it to the square: To call someone out for a fight.

Three knee deep: A shallow stab with a knife, not meant to kill but meant as a warning.

Three snap case: An unstable inmate who might go nuts without warning.

Tobacco: The hottest commodity (along with marijuana) in any prison, especially in the ones that ban smoking. Called by various names like "squares," "bales," "brown-eyed girl," tailor-mades.

Trailer/Trailer visit: A conjugal visit.

Viking: A sloppy prisoner who doesn't keep his cell or his body clean.

Wino time: A very short prison term. "Why he all trippin'? He ain't doin' nothin' but wino time, not like Smokey doin' 'all day and a night'!"

Wolf ticket: A prisoner or staffer who is all show and no action; a bluffer who acts tough but won't follow up if challenged. "He's selling wolf tickets."

Wood: White prisoner . . . a shortened version of "peckerwood."

World: The world outside the prison walls. "I made parole! I'm going back to the world!"

Yard: The exercise area. In some units it is just a square of concrete; in other units it may have grassy areas and basketball courts or weights.

X-Cat: A prisoner doing a life sentence.

ROOM WITH A BOO

Being of an adventurous, not to say foolish, spirit, I made arrangements to spend the night at San Antonio's Menger Hotel in a room that is rarely available to guests. The reason it is rarely available to guests is that people, both sane and otherwise, believe the room is haunted. I decided to stay there with nothing but a fistful of cigars and a Gideon Bible. I have to confess that as darkness descended outside, a gnawing feeling of foreboding descended upon my soul. But it was, I figured, the only way I'd have a ghost of a chance of seeing a ghost. I must admit that I was fairly cynical about the whole operation. That's probably the reason it wound up scaring the hell out of me.

Perhaps it was a blessing and a curse that the Menger Hotel was built upon the storied battlegrounds of the Alamo only twenty-three years after the fall of that bloody and beautiful cradle of Texas freedom. Be that as it may, since 1859 the Menger has been the home away from home to everybody from Robert E. Lee to Robert Mitchum to Robert Zimmerman. In 1976 I stayed at the Menger with Zimmerman, who is sometimes known as Bob Dylan, as part of his traveling musical circus, the Rolling Thunder Revue. Bob played his harmonica all night long, and when I finally got to sleep, I dreamed that I'd died and gone to heaven. I told Saint Peter that I wasn't coming in unless he promised that Bob wouldn't be there. He promised, I entered, and the next thing I heard was a familiar-sounding, whiny harmonica, which caused me to become highly *agitato* and accuse Saint Peter of welshing. Saint Peter, already mildly miffed by my presence, then intoned, "I'm telling you, hoss, that's not Bob Dylan. That's God. He just thinks He's Bob Dylan."

Be that as it may, a galaxy of other luminaries—from Oscar Wilde to John Wayne—has stayed at the Menger as well. Teddy Roosevelt organized the Rough Riders at the Menger Bar in 1898. It has been widely reported that on one fateful night Teddy's monocle popped out and fell into his jug of Old Grand-Dad, which he promptly drank, monocle and all. It gave him some new insights into himself— eventually leading him to run for the presidency. In all, a grand total of thirteen presidents and future presidents have spent time at the Menger over the years, including Bill Clin-

> "I'm telling you, hoss, that's not Bob Dylan. That's God. He just thinks He's Bob Dylan."
> —SAINT PETER

ton, who stopped by to sample the hotel's famous mango ice cream, and Bush the Younger, who in those days may very likely have stopped by to sample a little of what made Teddy want to run for president.

There have been other guests at the Menger who are not as celebrated. They make spontaneous appearances, never bothering to call ahead for reservations and seldom, if ever, staying the night. They arrive in the form of spirits from the near and distant past. For want of a better term, they are widely regarded as some of the world's best-documented, most-often-sighted, most highly discerning ghosts.

Probably the most reliable authority of these ghostly comings and goings is Ernesto L. Malacara, who's been with the hotel for twenty-four years. Ernesto has fielded hundreds of reports about the apparitions and has been an eyewitness as well. Not long ago in the spacious Victorian lobby, Ernesto saw what he at first thought was a homeless woman. Upon closer inspection, he noticed that her lace-up leather shoes, high-collared dress, and John Denver glasses were not the sartorial choices of the day. When he asked if she was all right, she looked up with the strangest, most ice-blue eyes and told him she was fine. He then walked about five steps away, turned around, and of course, she was gone.

There are two rooms in the Menger into which some maids will enter only in pairs, like animals at Noah's ark, because of recurrent ghostly activity. There have been a number of sightings of Captain Richard King, the founder of the King Ranch, who liked the hotel so much he died there in 1885. The front desk occasionally receives late-night inquiries from guests regarding a maid wearing a lace apron who ignores them. The desk always tells the guests the same thing: "Maids haven't worn those lace uniforms in eighty years."

Maybe it was the combination of Old Grand-Dad and mango ice cream, but I woke up from a little power nap at 3:17 in the morning and knew that something was wrong. A beautiful young woman with a bandanna around her head was floating at the foot of my bed. She did not look like Willie Nelson, and I knew it wasn't a dream. I sat bolt upright and shook my head vigorously in a vain effort to will the vision away. She began swaying slightly and motioning at me with her hands and her dark, flashing eyes. It was definitely time to leap sideways. After I hopped out of bed, I followed her across the room, where, after a two-and-a-half-minute eternity, she floated into the wall and disappeared.

> Maybe it was the combination of Old Grand-Dad and mango ice cream, but I woke up from a little power nap at 3:17 in the morning and knew that something was wrong.
>
> ◆
>
> But what are ghosts after all, if not the spirits of those we have loved and those we have lost and, just possibly, those we have yet to discover?

At dawn, I called Ernesto. "That's our Sallie," he told me cheerfully. "Our Sallie?" I asked. "She's probably our most frequently sighted ghost," he explained. "Sallie White was a pretty mulatto chambermaid at the hotel. She often tied her hair back with a bandanna." This made me a little nervous in the service; I had not told Ernesto that fact. "And she was shot by her jealous husband," he said, "on March 28, 1876."

Maybe it was just wishful thinking, but the flickering images of Sallie White seemed to remind me of an old flame. Her name was Jo Thompson, and she was Miss Texas in 1987. The two of us had had a good deal in common, of course, since I was Miss Texas in 1967. Nevertheless, there were striking similarities between the unforgettably radiant young countenances of Jo and Sallie. Everyone sees what they want to see, I suppose. I miss Miss Texas. I've often wondered what might have happened to the two of us if the world hadn't gotten in the way. But what are ghosts after all, if not the spirits of those we have loved and those we have lost and, just possibly, those we have yet to discover?

PART III

YESTERDAY STREET

KEEP GOMORRAH
WEIRD

———————◆———————

In the fifties, I moved from Houston to Austin, which didn't seem like that much of a cataclysmic cultural leap at the time. Compared to Houston, Austin was a sleepy, beautiful little town in which I went to high school and formed my first band, the Three Rejects. It would take another decade or two for Austin to become fully vilified by the rest of Texas as the long-haired, hippie, pot-smoking, hell-raising Gomorrah of the Western World. I never felt this way about Austin. All I knew was that the music was great, the drugs were cheap, and the love was free.

When I enrolled in the University of Texas, Willie Nelson was still a struggling songwriter and pig farmer in Nashville, and the Armadillo World Headquarters was just a gleam in Eddie Wilson's eye. In college, I distinguished myself by managing my friend Ken Jacobs's nearly successful campaign for head cheerleader in which our slogan was "I can jump high." I also formed my second band, King Arthur and the Carrots. I met folksingers, poets, political radicals, and women who loved other women. None of these life choices was in mainstream fashion, of course. Back then, I never could have used the slogan for my white-hot gubernatorial campaign: "No lesbian left behind."

> All I knew was that the music was great, the drugs were cheap, and the love was free.

In my bright college days, we pretty much took for granted that Austin was far more progressive than the outlying provinces. Looking back, I'm not so sure that was entirely true. In the early sixties there was a place called the Plantation Restaurant at the corner of the Drag and what was then Nineteenth Street. It was open twenty-four hours, many of which were spent by me and my friends drinking endless cups of blue coffee and solving the problems of the world as we knew it—and I think that, at times, we very possibly knew the world better then than we know it now. One thing that didn't really seem to register at the ol' Plantation, however, was that, among the bikers, fraternity boys, and square dance clubs, there were no black patrons. It took me a while, but as a card-carrying member of Students for a Democratic Society, I finally lamped upon this inequity. With my fellow SDSers, we picketed night after night, at last forcing the restaurant to change its policies. Today the Plantation, which I both loved and protested against, is gone, and the street where it used to be is no longer known

CALLAHAN

as Nineteenth Street. It is now called Martin Luther King Boulevard. In a world of shopping malls and glass towers, that, my friends, is real progress.

After graduation, I left Austin for three years to work in the Peace Corps in the jungles of Borneo. By the time I returned, there was an almost palpable new spirit in the air, what Jack London might have called "the smoke of life." Not that Austin wasn't an exciting place before I left, but now it really seemed to rock. I blame this transformation mostly on Willie. He likes to say that he just "found a parade and jumped in front of it." The truth is that when Willie began playing the Armadillo in the early 1970s, the union was finally consummated between the long-haired, dope-smoking hippie and the cowboy, giving birth almost simultaneously to the Cosmic Cowboy and the Outlaw Movement, and giving God-fearing folks who'd never trusted Austin in the first place a real reason to worry.

Willie was not alone, of course. Other cosmic cowboys like Waylon Jennings, Doug Sahm, Michael Murphy, Billy Joe Shaver, Steve Fromholtz, Jerry Jeff Walker, and Ray Wylie Hubbard also led the charge. And somewhere in there was a wiry little band called Kinky Friedman and the Texas Jewboys. But it was ten minutes after "Blue Eyes Cryin' in the Rain" exploded on the national consciousness that everybody wanted to come to Austin to have their hip cards punched. And the converted National Guard armory known as the Armadillo World Headquarters was just the place. No seats. No air-conditioning. No pretense. It was too late to stop the train. And that was a good thing, because you never know which one might be the train to glory.

I have recently written a guide to Austin called *The Great Psychedelic Armadillo Picnic*. It's a big title for a rather small book, but in the process of researching and writing it, I once again discovered the reasons God made Austin the Live Music

> **It was ten minutes after "Blue Eyes Cryin' in the Rain" exploded on the national consciousness that everybody wanted to come to Austin to have their hip cards punched.**
>
> ◆
>
> **Most of the Austin I used to know, along with most of my mind, is gone like the now-extinct blue-buttocked tropical loon.**

Capital of the World. I relived a moonlit night with a long-ago high school sweetheart, parked on top of Mount Bonnell in my 1953 green Plymouth Cranbrook convertible complete with wolf whistle and Bermuda bell. She left me for a quarterback even though I held the vaunted position of sports editor of the Austin High newspaper, the *Austin Maroon,* in which I once published a review of a football game in Latin. Poor girl never realized she could've been the future first lady of Texas.

Most of the Austin I used to know, however, along with most of my mind, is gone like the now-extinct blue-buttocked tropical loon. Some of the greatest times of my life were lived right here in this open-minded, open-hearted, much-maligned, much-celebrated, magical town. In the jukebox of my dreams I have vivid early memories of Willie, and Jerry Jeff, and Doug along with so many others—moments of fine madness, high lonesome nights, running and playing together like the kids we were when all the pearls were in the ocean and all the stars were in the sky.

> As old Austinites used to say: Onward through the fog.

Today, as I sit on the deck of my family's home on Mountainclimb Drive, I can clearly recall a vanished vista of rolling green hills, replaced by a glut of new houses, the bigger the better, as far as the eye can see. The city has become more high-tech now, more conservative, some say, more California-influenced. But underneath, I know the old DNA is still there. Since my father's death two years ago, I find myself hanging around Austin even more than usual. Like the deer that now populate Mountainclimb, I relish those rare moments of peace that life and love and leaf-blowers occasionally bestow. Like the deer, I'm caught in the headlights of the twenty-first century, somewhere between progress and the world we used to know.

In the meantime, I do my best to keep Austin weird. As old Austinites used to say: Onward through the fog.

PSYCHO PATHS

—————— ◆ ——————

This, gentile reader, is a tale of two Eagle Scouts. One was Charles Joseph Whitman, who, in 1966, climbed the Tower at the University of Texas and shot forty-five people.

The other is my mild-mannered friend, Brian D. Sweany. Both loved the Boy Scouts, both attended large Texas universities, both married beautiful blonde women, and both had dogs and guns. Indeed, the only discernible difference between the two is that my friend hasn't shot more than forty people—yet. Nevertheless, I usually avoid getting into tension conventions with Brian. He is, after all, an Eagle Scout.

Why is this important? Because I believe there is something in the mind-set of the Eagle Scout that provides an excellent breeding ground for the future mass murderers of America.

Maybe it's that, while the rest of us are desperately trying to extricate ourselves from a turbulent and troubling adolescence, the Eagle Scout is assiduously applying himself to the narrow, maddening craft of knot tying. It's my theory that in a universe of Eagle Scouts, you'd find an extremely high proportion of psychopaths. I can't prove my theory, because I don't have a computer nor am I ever likely to have one. If some geeky ten-year-old has a little time on his hands, it might be helpful to establish the statistical link between Eagle Scouts and mass murderers. Once this is done, all we'd have to do is send all the Eagle Scouts to Eagle Pass for a lucid-dreaming seminar.

> I believe there is something in the mind-set of the Eagle Scout that provides an excellent breeding ground for the future mass murderers of America.

Back in the sixties, I did pen an infamous little ditty about that murderous Eagle Scout. It's called "The Ballad of Charles Whitman." If you like, I can hum a few bars:

He was sittin' up there for more than an hour,
Way up there on the Texas Tower,
Shooting from the twenty-seventh floor.
He didn't choke or slash or slit them,
Not our Charles Joseph Whitman.
He won't be an architect no more.
Got up that morning calm and cool.
He picked up his guns and walked to school.
All the while he smiled so sweetly,

"Just when I thought things couldn't get any worse!"

Then he blew their minds completely.
They'd never seen an Eagle Scout so cruel.
There was a rumor about a tumor
Nestled at the base of his brain.
He was sitting up there with his .36 Magnum,
Laughin' wildly as he bagged 'em.
Who are we to say the boy's insane?

Of course, I'm wary of more than just Eagle Scouts. Another pet theory of mine deals with people who have the name
"Wayne."

I believe we should keep an eye on these folks. Most of them are up to no good. The problem, I contend, begins at birth when the father, invariably a fan of John Wayne, blithely borrows the name for his son. The son, no doubt, cannot live up to the John Wayne lifestyle and may indeed prefer to be an interior decorator subsisting almost entirely on banana bread and Brie. This irritates the macho father to no end and causes a deep guilt to fester in the young man, until one day he snaps his wig completely and swerves to hit a school bus. Examples of the Wayne Phenomenon are legion: John Wayne Gacy, Elmer Wayne Henley, John Wayne Nobles, Wayne Williams, Michael Wayne McGray, Christopher Wayne Lippard, Dennis Wayne Eaton, and Wayne Nance, merry mass murderers and serial killers all.

> Another pet theory of mine deals with people who have the name "Wayne."
>
> ◆
>
> "Sometimes he thinks he's John Wayne."
> —JOHN FORD

Personally, I have nothing against John Wayne, and I don't believe that the Duke's impossibly high macho standard should be held against him. It's not his fault that a statistically significant number of screwed-up young men bearing his name struggle to please their equally misguided fathers. Even John Ford, who was a friend of Wayne's and directed a number of his movies, became a little nervous in the service when working with the Duke. "Sometimes," said Ford, "he thinks he's John Wayne."

Wayne, of course, was not from Texas, but he acted like he was. Texas has always had a lot to brag about, and one area of

PSYCHO PATHS — 109

which we're particularly proud, is the many mass murderers who were born in the Lone Star State. There's Richard Speck, who killed eight nurses in Chicago. He was a sick chicken and then he took a turn for the nurse. And don't forget Charles "Tex" Watson, Charlie Manson's executive butt boy (never trust a guy named "Tex") and Henry Lee Lucas, who killed about 400 million people but can't remember where he buried the bodies. Occasionally, no doubt, Texans tend to get a bit overzealous, and we brag about

> As a Tower guard told me years later: "It'll happen to you."

murders that aren't even our own, so to speak. The Texas Chainsaw Massacre is a good example. It's loosely based on an incident that took place in Wisconsin.

But Charles Whitman (Charles Watson, Charles Manson— could be something here) was one of the first modern mass murderers. On the surface, he was just an ex-Marine sharpshooter, who may have been studying too hard in the stacks— until he blew his own stack. As a Tower guard told me years later: "It'll happen to you."

"The Ballad of Charles Whitman" closes with the following verse:

The doctors tore his poor brain down,
But not a snitch of illness could be found.
Most folks couldn't figure just why he did it,
And them that could would not admit it.
There's still a lot of Eagle Scouts around.

FALLEN EAGLES

Not every boy who joins a Boy Scout troop earns the Eagle Scout rank; only about 4 percent of all Boy Scouts do so. This represents more than one million Boy Scouts who have earned the rank since 1911. Nevertheless, the goals of Scouting—citizenship training, character development, and personal fitness—remain important for all Scouts, whether or not they attain the Eagle Scout rank.

That said, why do so many Eagle Scouts go bad? I'm not saying that all Eagle Scouts take a walk on the dark side; billionaire H. Ross Perot was an Eagle Scout as was Lloyd M. Bentsen Jr., former Secretary of the Treasury and former Texas senator. Both men have lived honorable lives, but what accounts for the fallen Eagles like Charles Manson in Los Angeles and Daniel Altstadt, the axe murderer from San Diego?

CALLAHAN

"DADDY, TELL US ABOUT THE TIME YOU KILLED US ALL IN A SUICIDAL RAGE!"

Why are so many Eagle Scouts on death row? The Boy Scouts don't allow non-Christians or gays in their organization. You would think that would weed out the nutters but apparently not.

Below is a look at the dark side of Eagle Scouting . . . the fallen Eagles from Texas.

CHARLES WHITMAN: On a hot August day in 1966, U.S. Marine and former Eagle Scout Charles Whitman climbed the clock tower at the University of Texas and spent ninety-two minutes picking off pedestrians with a sniper rifle. Earlier that day he had stabbed both his wife and mother to death in their homes. By the time the Austin PD finally killed Whitman, he had murdered sixteen and wounded thirty-one.

LESLEY LEE GOSCH, former Eagle Scout, shot Rebecca Jo Patton, the wife of a bank president, in the head six times with a handgun as part of a failed extortion plot. Patton's two daughters, ages eleven and fifteen, found their mother dead in the hallway of their home in Alamo Heights, Texas. Gosch was sentenced to receive the death penalty while his partner in crime made a deal with the prosecuter and got off with forty-five years with the possibility of parole. Texas currently does not have a "life without parole" option. While on death row, Gosch took up art and twice asked for clemency, and was denied both times. After spending thirteen years on the row, Gosch was executed by lethal injection on April 4, 1998.

RON SCOTT SHAMBURGER: Shamburger and Lori Baker were fellow students at Texas A&M University. As freshmen, the two had gone dancing together, but years had passed before they saw each other again. In the fall of 1994, Shamburger went to Lori's home with a gun, gas can, and duct tape. He broke into the home through a window in a spare bedroom, then broke into Lori's locked bedroom where she slept. After Lori recognized Shamburger, he bound her hands with the duct tape. At this point, Lori's roommate, Victoria

Kohler, returned home. Once Shamburger heard Victoria enter, he placed the pistol against Lori's head and shot her. (Shamburger had burglarized the home a week earlier, stealing Lori's credit card, which he used to purchase the murder weapon.)

Shamburger then abducted Victoria, tied her up, put her in the trunk of a car, and drove around town. He then abandoned the car, went back to Lori's house, and set it on fire. Before doing so, he used a knife to cut into Baker's head in an attempt to find the bullet and remove it. When he failed, he poured gasoline on her body and set the house on fire. As the blaze expanded, the house eventually exploded. Shamburger later confessed to his minister, and then to police. In September 2002, Shamburger was executed by lethal injection in Texas. His final meal included nachos with chili and cheese, one bowl of sliced jalapenos, one bowl of picante sauce, two large onions, sliced and grilled, tacos with fresh tomatoes, lettuce, and cheese, and toasted corn tortilla shells.

RYAN JAMES FRAZIER: Students acquainted with this nineteen-year-old Baylor University freshman and former Eagle Scout saw him as an intelligent, quiet scholar who never lost his temper. When police arrested Frazier and charged him with murdering his parents and seventeen-year-old brother outside Victoria, Texas, people were stunned.

ROBERT DANIEL MURRAY: An Eagle Scout who was sentenced to seven years in prison for beating fifty-six-year-old Laura White with a metal pipe inside a Mormon church in Longview, Texas.

BRANDON SMITH, a sixteen-year-old Eagle Scout, and three of his friends set fire to Wylie Junior High School, causing $1.5 million in damages. He was later tried as an adult and sentenced to nine years in prison.

DOES NOT COMPUTE

———————◆———————

Dude, you're getting a Dell! You may be going to hell, but at least you'll be able to take your computer with you. You see, I believe the Internet is the work of Satan. As far as I can tell, this seductive spider web of insanity has only two possible functions. One is to connect a short, fat sixty-five-year-old man in New Jersey who's pretending to be a tall, young Norwegian chap to a vice cop in San Diego who's pretending to be a fifteen-year-old girl. The other purpose of this international network is to establish, once and for all, who is everybody's favorite Star Trek captain.

> **I believe the Internet is the work of Satan.**

Needless to say, I've never used the Internet, owned a computer, or had an e-mail address. Then again, why would anybody with a brain the size of a small Welsh mining town ever need those things? If you require information on a certain subject, go to one of those places, I forget what you call them, with a lot of books inside and two lions out front. Pick a title, sit on the steps, and read between the lions. This may seem like a rather Neanderthal method of education, but at least you won't be tempted to pretend to be someone you're not and you won't get carpal tunnel syndrome. In fact, the only things you're liable to get are a little bit of knowledge and some pigeon droppings on your coat—which most people will tell you, and most computers won't—means good luck.

Good luck, of course, is better than a good hard drive anytime. I'm not really sure what a hard drive is, but I've heard grown-ups speak of it in positive tones. I've always found it ridiculous to hear people talk about how expensive, sophisticated, fast, or small their computers are. There must be something Freudian here, but I don't know what it is. I'm sure Freud himself didn't know what a hard drive was since he'd never even been up to Amarillo.

Of course, one reason I don't use a computer is because I'm too much of a genius to learn how. In fact, I write on the last typewriter in Texas. I think that computers contribute to the homogenization of everyone's brain. The technological revolution is not bringing us closer together—it's merely making us more the same. I have this archaic idea that you should try to get it right the first time. And if you don't, you should tear out the page and throw it in the fire. If you know you can change everything with some kind of electronic mouse, you'll never know what it's like to fly without the magic feather.

You'll never feel like Oscar Wilde behind bars with his hair on fire. Even Oscar had trouble with this sometimes. Maybe technology could have saved him. Maybe he could have called Emily Dickinson from a pay phone in the rain. Maybe Davy Crockett could have e-mailed Sylvia Plath from inside the Alamo, and she wouldn't have had to put her head inside the oven. But technology can't save everybody, and it may not be able to save anybody. There's no time between the windmill and the world to buy a van Gogh, to help Mozart out of the gutter, Sharansky out of the gulag, Rosa out of the back of the bus, or Anne out of the attic.

The other night I got home from a rather extended road trip and found that lightning had struck the dish, which meant I couldn't watch *Matlock*. I figured I'd listen to a little music, maybe some Beethoven or Roger Miller. You can imagine my chagrin when I walked over and discovered that the cat had vomited on my CD player. Now I was forced to take the fifth on Beethoven. It was Roger and out. Without even the rudimentary elements of technological input in my life, I was truly back to the basics. There was nothing to do but think. Nothing to do but dream. Nothing to do but remember.

I recalled a small incident that had occurred earlier that afternoon when I'd walked into one of those OfficeMax places

> **Freud himself didn't know what a hard drive was since he'd never been up to Amarillo.**
>
> ◆
>
> **There's no time between the windmill and the world to buy a van Gogh, to help Mozart out of the gutter, Sharansky out of the gulag, Rosa out of the back of the bus, or Anne out of the attic.**

in Kerrville like a mad scientist, searching desperately for a cartridge that might mate harmoniously with the last typewriter in Texas. Of course, I didn't find it. As I was leaving in a snit, I saw an old-timer entering the place, carefully clutching what is now considered an antique, a hand-levered calculator. He was a tiny man with a long white beard and a crushed straw hat on his wizened head. He wasn't getting a Dell. He was just hoping that the young techno wizards at OfficeMax could repair his calculator.

"It's not even in the catalog!" the tall, impossibly young salesman crowed almost joyously. Other employees crowded around to voice similar expressions of amazement bordering upon ridicule over this piece of machinery that had once been a workhorse of American business. "This belongs in a museum!" they laughed. But it wasn't a museum piece to the old man, who carried it protectively out into the parking lot. I looked up at the garish chain store in the ugly strip mall in the little town that was growing increasingly similar to every other town. Something there is that doesn't love a mall, I thought. Something.

Back at the house that night, with the cat vomit slowly drying on the CD player, I sat back and lit up a cigar. I blew a smoke ring. It wasn't perfect, but it wasn't bad. I remembered how my old pal Wavy Gravy used to salute mistakes and imperfections. He said that's what made us human. Meanwhile, that obnoxious kid was back on TV, smiling satanically at me like some adolescent Ronald Reagan pitchman, telling me I'm getting a Dell. I don't want a Dell. I just want a typewriter cartridge. And the next time that kid says, "Dude, you're getting a Dell," I want a windmill to fall on him.

IF THE TEN COMMANDMENTS WERE WRITTEN BY A TEXAN . . .

1. Thou shalt hold no other state or country above Texas.
2. Thou shalt worship the shape of the Lone Star State and thou shalt make everything in its image, from Texas-shaped pasta to Texas-shaped swimming pools.
3. Thou shalt have no other sport but football and no other professional team but the Cowboys.
4. Thou shalt own as many guns as thou dog hast fleas.
5. Honor thy styling gel, for it shall bring you great big hair.
6. Thou shalt say the word "Texas" as much as thee can, even when it is redundant to do so. For example, Austin should be said "Austin, Texas," even if thee

standeth on the Capitol steps beneath a sign that says "Austin, Texas." Fear not overuse of the word "Texas" for such a thing is not possible.

7. Thou shalt keep Friday night sacred for that is when thy high school football team playest. Schedule not births, weddings, funerals, or baptisms on this holy day, for Friday nights are reserved to paint thy face in team colors and feast on roasted turkey legs during halftime.

8. Honor thy dog, for he will be loyal unto thee even when the oil wells dry up and the last beer is consumed.

9. Thou shalt consume no other carbonated beverage but Dr Pepper.

10. Thou shalt not covet thy neighbor's mud flaps.

THE JEST IS HISTORY

The fabled, long-lost Beaumont Scrolls, rumored to have been written by Bubba Nostradamus and clandestinely passed along for generations at otherwise stultifyingly dull Rotary Club meetings, have at last been found! The B.S., as they are sometimes referred to by biblical scholars, were discovered recently by workmen excavating the site for a new Taco Bell. The scrolls tell us that God created Texas in six days and six nights, and on the seventh day He rested and played a few rounds of miniature golf. On the eighth day, He created the rest of the world and then hunkered down at Saint Peter's Garden of Eatin' with a chicken-fried steak and some rather heavenly cream gravy. God said the chicken-fried steak was good.

Though He devoted most of His time to Texas, the de-

mands of being the CEO of all creation caused Him to over-
look a few details. Maybe He deemed them too insignificant,
or maybe He just didn't like to delegate. We're talking about

spiritual trivia like giant mosqui-

> God said the chicken-
> fried steak was good.

toes in Lufkin, hungry horseflies in
Bandera, murderous traffic in Houston, and the fact that some folks
have wandered forty years in the

desert trying to get a hotel room in Dallas. Most scholars of
the Beaumont Scrolls, however, believe these obvious over-
sights to have been intentional. God, they say, fully meant to
afflict generations of Texans with these plagues. It was the
only way He could think of to remind them that they were
merely human.

By 325 B.C., Alexander the Great had conquered much of
the known world. Alex was short, very much distrusted cats
and newspapers, and had never even heard of Texas. Meanwhile, the Greeks began experimenting with diet hemlock
and nude javelin throwing, the Romans were eating large
amounts of Caesar salad and building deeper vomitoriums,
and the Trojans were practicing safe sex while trying not to
look a gift horse in the mouth. None of these people had ever
heard of Texas either.

Back in the Lone Star State, a rich and colorful history
was evolving. Hundreds of years before pale men arrived on
floating houses, the human landscape was dominated by two
rather primitive Indian tribes, the Neimans and the Mucuses. Since people in those days often forgot to make reservations, the two tribes built their casinos and campfires on

opposite sides of a large lake. The Neimans hated the Mucuses and the Mucuses hated the Neimans. The Mucuses became so sick of the Neimans poking fun at their name that
they eventually had it officially changed to "Marcus." Both
tribes kept pretty much to themselves, and nobody bothered
them because nobody even knew they existed, except possibly James Michener. It is said that a young Neiman named
Horny Toad fell in love with a pretty Marcus girl named Little Mud Hen and that one moonlit night the two of them
swam far out to the middle of the lake, embraced each other,
and vanished beneath the waves. Centuries later, white
tourists would bore Indian guides into a coma by incessantly
inquiring about the legend. The Indian guides would duly
repeat the story, after which the tourists would invariably

ask, "What do you call this lake?" The Indians would respond, "We call it Lake Stupid."

Not long after Columbus discovered the Bank of America, de Soto discovered the Mississippi River and later had a car named after him. In 1541, Coronado claimed Texas for the King of Spain, who was out burning witches and missed Coronado's call. The two reportedly played phone tag for almost twenty years. Nevertheless, Coronado had a car—and a recreational vehicle—named after him. More than a century passed before the French explorer La Salle, through an error in his global positioning system, mistook Matagorda Bay for the mouth of the Mississippi. He also had a car named after him. French influence was never strong in Texas, mostly because of language difficulties. While Texans had no problem pronouncing the word "awl," they could never quite seem to correctly enunciate the word "beignet."

By the time the Mexicans attacked the Alamo in 1836, the Texans had already absorbed so much multicultural influence they decided to build a theme park. They called it Three Flags Over Texas. It was successful for a while but then had to declare Chapter 11. More than a century later, cult leader David Koresh at-

> Hundreds of years before pale men arrived on floating houses, the human landscape was dominated by two rather primitive Indian tribes, the Neimans and the Mucuses.
>
> Not long after Columbus discovered the Bank of America, de Soto discovered the Mississippi River and later had a car named after him.

tempted to build a similar theme park near Waco. It was called 666 Flags Over Texas. It also failed. The Alamo, however, survived as an icon to the world. People marveled at how a small band of men could have held out for so long against Santa Anna. People also wondered how the defenders could have survived for thirteen whole days without the benefit of fax machines.

The B.S. tell us that the two Indian tribes, the Neimans and the Marcuses, eventually got together and opened a large department store in Dallas. Neiman Marcus, it is revealed, was the last place Jack Ruby shopped before he shot Lee Harvey Oswald. We are told that Ruby purchased a custom-made pair of red-white-and-blue boxer shorts emblazoned with the strangely prophetic, almost visionary words: "Hot babes! Cold beer! Nuke 'em, W!" The B.S., however, do not tell us what will happen to the Dallas Cowboys. They don't tell us what will happen to the rest of us either.

As far as Jack Ruby is concerned, controversy has swirled around this shadowy, flamboyant figure for decades. Was Ruby a true American hero? Was he a minor player in the JFK tragedy? Was he a pawn of the Mafia? The only thing the Beaumont Scrolls tell us is that he did not have a car named after him.

YESTERDAY STREET

———◆———

Growing up in Houston in the fifties now seems a magical, oblivious moment that shines through the traffic-clogged world of today and lingers like a love affair from one's youth. As kids at Edgar Allan Poe Elementary School, my little friends and I quite possibly did not realize or appreciate that Houston was one of the hottest, most humid places in the civilized world, teeming with mosquitoes and oil-rich right-wingers, stunted by polio and segregation, blessed with banana splits and Christmas tree forts. We just thought of it as home. For some of us, it's still home. For others, it is a place we once loved that has long since become a station on the way.

Yesterday Street for me was 2635 Nottingham, in West University Place, where my mother took me swimming at Shakespeare's Pool, our maid made popcorn balls, and my dad taught me to play chess. He taught me well enough that in 1952, at the age of seven, I was a prodigy of sorts, though it has been rather downhill from there. That was the year when I, along with about fifty adults, took on the world grand master, Samuel Reshevsky, in a simultaneous marathon match in a hotel that I'm sure is now a Bennigan's. In an hour and a half, Reshevsky beat all of us. I, by far his youngest opponent, wound up with my picture on page one of the *Houston Chronicle*. Afterward, Reshevsky told my dad that he was sorry to have beaten me, but he had to be especially careful with young kids. "To be beaten by anyone under eleven," he said, "would be headlines."

> Houston was teeming with mosquitoes and oil-rich right-wingers, stunted by polio and segregation, blessed with banana splits and Christmas tree forts.

Not long after I lost to Reshevsky, Adlai Stevenson lost to Ike (except for my family, everybody in Houston liked Ike); Hank Williams died in the backseat of a Cadillac on his way to a gig in Canton, Ohio (some people will do anything to get out of a gig in Canton, Ohio); Julius and Ethel Rosenberg were executed by our government as spies for the Soviet Union; and a ten-year-old boy named Ken Ford got a new BB gun for Christmas. Ken lived in a faraway galaxy at the other end of Nottingham. One afternoon, when my dad was at work, Ken came over to our house and began shooting birds in our front yard. I wanted him to stop, but he wouldn't, and he was a bigger kid, so I couldn't make him. By the time my dad got home, the lawn was littered with the tiny bodies of dead birds. My dad got out of his car wearing black pleated trousers, a white shirt open at the collar, and an unusually grim expression. He asked Ken if the gun was his and if he could see it. Ken said yes and proudly handed it to my father, who, with righteous fury, broke it over his knee into two pieces and, without saying a word, handed them to the boy.

Speaking of righteous fury, the principal of Edgar Allan Poe was a devoutly religious woman whom we would probably call a fundamentalist today. Back then, all we knew was that Mrs. Doty devoted a hugely inordinate amount of class time to rehearsing for the Christmas pageant. I participated in this elaborate mandatory religious festival in the third grade, but by the fourth grade I was boycotting. While the rest of the school was busy rehearsing, I stayed in the classroom alone and wrote poems. One of them was about our librarian, an attractive young woman named Miss Barrett, who told us she couldn't sleep at night, because she could hear every little sound outside on the street. The poem went as follows:

> "To be beaten by anyone under eleven," he said, "would be headlines."
> —SAMUEL RESHEVSKY

The very best eyesight there ever was
Was accomplished by eating carrots.
But the very best hearing on earth by far
Is sure to be Miss Barrett's.

Mrs. Doty did not find my work amusing, and I'm sure she believed I was going to hell. God eventually punished her by causing her to fall off the stage at the Christmas pageant and break her leg.

God punished me by putting me through the absolute hell of adolescence. By age twelve, even private jitterbug lessons administered by our neighbor Susan Kaufman had failed to save me from teenage spiritual leprosy. At thirteen, I was bar mitzvahed by Rabbi Robert I. Kahn at Temple Emanu El, and my Torah portion dealt with Jacob's ladder. I only truly began to climb that ladder, I felt, the following year, when I walked into the Bell School of Music on Edloe Street, canceled my accordion lessons, and traded in my accordion for a guitar. The first song I learned to play was "Fraulein," by Bobby Helms. I didn't know it then, but there was another kid in Houston who was just picking up the guitar around that time, and the first song he learned was also "Fräulein." I met him twenty years later. His name was Townes Van Zandt. My girlfriend was Bunny Slipakoff, a fräulein I did not learn to play, thereby setting the pattern for all future relationships. My favorite restaurant was Prince's Drive-In, where you called in your order on a telephone and it was delivered on roller skates.

> By age twelve, even private jitterbug lessons administered by our neighbor Susan Kaufman had failed to save me from teenage spiritual leprosy.

A lot of years have rolled by since then. Upon reflection, I see that the Houston I grew up in was a vibrant city not without charm, a colorful, soulful, independent-minded place. The inhabitants, no doubt, could probably only dimly envision the big-city future into which they would inexorably be dragged, some of them kicking and screaming, some quite willingly. I don't know what became of Susan Kaufman or Mrs. Doty or Ken Ford. Sometimes, when I visit briefly on book tours, I'm not even sure what became of Houston. It now seems like every other large American city—the same suburbs, the same stores, the same restaurants. Starbucks is springing up everywhere.

Somewhere between the smog and the Southwest Freeway, I know old Buffalo Bayou is still there, the lifeblood of the city, flowing valiantly through the veins of a dying junkie standing at the corner of youth and vermouth with a sign that reads, NEED FUEL FOR LEAR JET.

★ PART IV ★

THE
REDHEADED
STRANGER

THE WANDERER

With the possible exception of a few early serial killers, Jerry Jeff Walker was one of the first people in America to pioneer and popularize the three-word name. I've often maintained that if Susan Walker, Jerry Jeff's wife/manager (emphasis on slash), had married me instead of him, I'd be the president of the United States and he would be sleeping under a bridge. While this may not be entirely true, it is accurate to say that Jerry Jeff would no doubt be very happy sleeping under a bridge. Especially if you let him have his guitar.

Jerry Jeff is not only a Texas music icon, he's something even more important to me: a friend. When I needed help in my 1986 campaign for justice of the peace in Kerrville, Jerry Jeff was there. When the Utopia Animal Rescue Ranch held its first "benefit," in 1999, Jerry Jeff was our headliner. I've called upon Jerry Jeff so often, in fact, that Susan once asked him, "Doesn't Kinky know any other celebrities?" I do, but few of them are as generous with their time. That's why I was happy to comply several years ago when he asked me to give him a blurb for his autobiography, *Gypsy Songman*. Now that I'm digging deeper into Jerry Jeff's life, I find myself in that most ironic of karmic circumstances: having to actually read a book I've given a blurb for. And you know something? It's pretty damn good.

> I find myself in that most ironic of karmic circumstances: having to actually read a book I've given a blurb for.

Way back when doctors drove Buicks, Jerry Jeff rode his thumb out of his hometown in upstate New York, stopped by Key West long enough to invent Jimmy Buffett, then drifted over to New Orleans, where he sang for pennies on street corners. Perhaps he was curious to discover, in the words of Bob Dylan, "Who's gonna throw that minstrel boy a coin?" Jerry Jeff remembers a time when a group of fraternity boys about his own age came by and started getting on his case. "Why don't you get a job?" one of them said. "You can't just wander around with that old guitar forever."

"Watch me," said Jerry Jeff.

In the mid-sixties, before he was nothing, as we used to say in Nashville, Jerry Jeff was singing in Austin. Today we would probably call him a homeless person with a guitar. During this period he wrote "Mr. Bojangles," a song that now resides comfortably among the most recorded songs of all time. Looking back, it is hard to believe that a record executive once passed on the song, remarking at the time, "Nobody wants to hear a song about an old drunk nigger and a dead dog."

"Mr. Bojangles was actually white," Jerry Jeff told me recently. "If he'd been black, I never would've met him. The prison was segregated."

"It's a perfect song," I said. "But you keep changing the melody and fooling with the phrasing. Why?"

"To discourage people from singing along."

I asked Jerry Jeff to tell me about writing "Mr. Bojangles." This is what he said: "I'd been reading a lot of Dylan Thomas, and I was really into the concept of internal rhyme. I just had my guitar, a yellow pad, and the memories of guys I'd met in drunk tanks and on the street—one gentle old man in particular. The rest of the country was listening to the Beatles, and I was writing a six-eight waltz about an old man and hope. It was a love song.

"During the time I was writing 'Mr. Bojangles,' I used to go down to the Austin city pound about every two weeks and adopt a dog. I didn't really live anywhere myself, so the dog would often stay with me awhile and then it would run away. Maybe find somebody else. At least I felt I was giving him a second chance."

> Way back when doctors drove Buicks, Jerry Jeff rode his thumb out of his hometown in upstate New York, stopped by Key West long enough to invent Jimmy Buffett, then drifted over to New Orleans, where he sang for pennies on street corners.
>
> ◆
>
> "Mr. Bojangles was actually white. If he'd been black, I never would've met him. The prison was segregated."
> —JERRY JEFF WALKER

Jerry Jeff got a second chance himself when he married Susan in 1974. She is largely credited with turning his life around and turning his career into a financial pleasure. Not only does he have houses in Austin, New Orleans, and Belize, but also, quite possibly for the first time in a lifetime of rambling, a sense of home. Jerry Jeff and Susan have two children, Jessie Jane and Django, who is starting to make a name for himself in the music world. Django has an album out and a hit song, "Texas on My Mind," that was recorded by Pat Green and Cory Morrow. The Walkers credit Django's attending Paul McCartney's Liverpool Institute for the Performing Arts with honing his skills as a songwriter and performer. They are currently in the final planning stages of opening a similar school in Austin. It will be, Susan says, a nonprofit organization of international scope, teaching music as well as the music business to anyone with the talent to gain admission.

> Through the music of Jerry Jeff Walker, people like Hondo Crouch, Charlie Dunn, and the ubiquitous Mr. Bojangles seem to live forever.

The school could someday provide young people from around the world with the kind of education, direction, and support that Jerry Jeff himself never had. His education and inspiration were often provided by the real-life characters he met on the street and on the road; he returned the favor by immortalizing many of them in his songs. Through the music of Jerry Jeff Walker, people like Hondo Crouch, Charlie Dunn, and the ubiquitous Mr. Bojangles seem to live forever. This is important, because people today don't often get the chance to meet such men in the halls and the malls of our modern-day world.

At a television taping in November, Jerry Jeff performed a few of these classics and then some songs by other songwriters. He played "The Cape," a song by Guy Clark about a kid who thinks he can fly. I've always found this song a trifle treacly, but that night it brought a tear to my eye. Then he played Ian Tyson's "Navajo Rug," which brought another tear, and Steve Fromholtz's "Singin' the Dinosaur Blues," which really started the waterworks. When "Redneck Mother," by Ray Wylie Hubbard, also put a tear in my eye, I realized that I was fairly heavily monstered.

Later, out on the street, I suddenly felt stone-cold sober. The ability to deliver another man's song faithfully is a rare enough talent, but Jerry Jeff Walker does not merely make a song his own. His magic is that he gives it to you.

THE WEDDING PARTYER

The last place you'd expect to begin a beautiful friendship with Pat Green would be at a Jewish wedding in Mexico City. But there he was, looking like the Jolly Green Giant, trying to open a bottle of tequila while repeatedly adjusting the yarmulke on his head. It was a strange sight, all right, but in this modern world, maybe not so strange. Pat and I, whom some might characterize as wedding guests from hell, had a mutual friend in the groom, Eddy Levy. Pat knew Eddy through the Texas music scene as the manager of Honeybrowne, a band he'd often played with. I knew Eddy and his brother Isaac as little boogers at my family's summer camp, Echo Hill.

The wedding was at the Four Seasons in Mexico City, one of the classiest, most lavish hotels in the world. Everywhere you go, there's the sound of rich people laughing. Pat is talented, intelligent, fun-loving, and humble, but his appearance can often be described as that of a big, sloppy Boy Scout with a merit badge in hell-raising—in other words, not your basic Four Seasons guest. That was fine with me. Every time I stay at a fancy hotel, some employee always comes up to me with deep suspicion in his eyes and says, "Can I help you?"

> Every time I stay at a fancy hotel, some employee always comes up to me with deep suspicion in his eyes and says, "Can I help you?"

As I was checking in on Friday morning, I could hear a loud, boisterous voice singing in a ballroom just off the lobby. People were shouting and laughing in both Spanish and English. My curiosity piqued, I thought I'd check it out before I checked in. I left my busted valise at the front desk and walked into the ballroom. There I saw a sight I shall not soon forget: Pat standing stubbornly like a giant statue of an Inca god, trying to play a serenade on a small guitar he'd "borrowed" from a determined little mariachi who was attempting to get it back. Like David and Goliath, the two of them struggled over the instrument, with the mariachi finally winning.

To smooth over any ill will, Pat proceeded to buy sixty-dollar shots of Don Julio Real tequila for everybody in the place. He bought so many rounds that the bartenders thought it was his birthday. Later, a large man was seen mooning people in the Four Seasons courtyard from his second-floor window. I'm not suggesting that the two events were related, but it's possible. Of course, after about eight shots of Don Julio Real, the man could have been me.

The ceremony itself, the following night, was a traditional one, performed entirely in Spanish and Hebrew, two languages that neither myself, nor Mr. Green Jeans, is fluent in. Unaware that a Mexican wedding party usually starts late and goes until dawn, we drank a good bit more Don Julio Real before, during, and after the ceremony. By the time Eddy and his lovely bride, Noa, entered the great hall as husband and wife, five hundred people were waving silk napkins over their heads, the band was playing, and Pat was kissing the father of the groom. We drank a lot more tequila and then were compelled at gunpoint to participate in an extended series of highly frenetic Jewish folk dances, which resulted in projectile vomiting and, from Pat, a few drunken words of wisdom.

"The problem with being drunk," he said, "is that you're drunk. And the problem with being in love is that you're drunk."

"That's pretty good," I said. "It ought to be a song."

"It will be," he said, "if I can just light this cigar."

"How does it feel to be playing your music to a crowd of fifty thousand?"

"It's exactly as cool as you think it is. The only reason they're there is because I can't put fifty thousand people in my house."

"I know how it feels," I said. "I've played to fifty thousand people before. Unfortunately, they were there to see Bob Dylan."

"Man, I love Bob Dylan."

"He speaks highly of you. You do appear to be taking your success as it comes. You're not going to allow yourself to turn into a brand name with nothing behind it, are you?"

Pat didn't respond directly, or maybe he did. It was hard to tell, because we were both making serious headway into another bottle of tequila. This is what my notebook tells me he said: "I've never met a man who was more or less important than me."

"Why is drinking so much a part of your life and your music?" I asked, rather rhetorically, as we both killed another shot.

"I don't like drinking songs," he said. "Just songs I can drink to. My dad says the key to a great love song is to never use the word 'love.' But back to drinking. Glen Campbell just got caught drinkin' and drivin'. Now, we're all bad drivers sooner or later. But I'm talkin' forgot-you-were-on-the-planet-Earth, left-your-kid-in-the-truck-stop-bathroom kind of drunk driving. He was arrested, and when they were taking his picture, he was singing his greatest hits to the camera. Now that's drunk. I've probably been there a time or two. But when I'm ready to leave a bar, I always ask myself the same question: 'Can I puke in a straight line?' "

> "When I'm ready to leave a bar, I always ask myself the same question: 'Can I puke in a straight line?' "
> —PAT GREEN
>
> ◆
>
> "His long suit is enjoying life rather than figuring it out."
> —CRAVEN GREEN

You couldn't help but like this guy, I thought. He was Pecos Bill from Texas Tech. He had mastered the art of being himself. Now he was working to a little larger audience, telling the story of how, in 1995, in Lubbock, he'd sneaked into Jerry Jeff Walker's dressing room just as the performer was coming offstage. "Hi, Mr. Walker," Pat said in an exaggerated drunken slur. "I'm Pat Green. I'm a Texas singer-songwriter. I've brought my favorite guitar for you to sign."

"What did Jerry Jeff say?" someone asked.

"He said, 'Take your favorite [expletive deleted] guitar and get out of my [expletive deleted] dressing room.' "

Let the history of Texas music record that Jerry Jeff did sign the young fan's guitar.

Later that night, much later, after the room stopped spinning, I thought about fame. "Death's little sister," Hemingway had called it. Pat seemed to be handling it very well, indeed. Something his father, Craven Green, a friend of mine, had once told me came to mind. "His long suit," Craven had said of his son, "is enjoying life rather than figuring it out." Craven told me the story of when he and Pat's mother were getting divorced. He'd bought a little book to explain to his two small boys that Mommy and Daddy still loved them. When he'd finished reading, both he and ten-year-old David were very torn up.

But six-year-old Pat's reaction was quite different. He put his arm around his father's neck. "Hey, Dad," he said, "it's not the end of the world."

THE TEXAS CELEBRITY CHEERLEADER HALL OF FAME

- **GEORGE W. BUSH:** A cheerleader at Phillips Academy, Andover, Massachusetts.

- **BETTY BUCKLEY:** Texas-born Broadway actress (*1776, Pippin, Cats*) and Hollywood star (*Tender Mercies*). Buckley was a head cheerleader at Texas Christian University; Buckley also won the title of Miss Fort Worth (1966) and was runner-up in the Miss Texas competition.

- **STEVE MARTIN:** Comedian and movie star from Waco, was a cheerleader in high school.

- **DWIGHT D. EISENHOWER:** Our thirty-fourth president, world-renowned general, and West Point cheerleader. From West Point, Eisenhower (via speaker phone) led an Academy pep rally the day before the anxiously awaited annual Army-Navy game, proving that at fifty-five, he was still West Point's most spirited cheerleader.

♦ SANDRA BULLOCK attended Arlington's Washington-Lee High School, where she was a cheerleader and was voted Most Likely to Brighten Your Day. She has starred in numerous movies including *Forces of Nature, Prince of Egypt, Practical Magic, Making Sandwiches, Hope Floats, Speed 2, In Love and War,* and *Time to Kill.*

♦ HELOISE: San Antonio native, syndicated columnist ("Heloise's Helpful Household Hints") and, of course, an ex-cheerleader.

♦ PHYLLIS GEORGE BROWN: Former cheerleader, CBS broadcaster, and 1971 Miss America; born in Denton in 1949 and attended North Texas State University.

♦ AARON SPELLING: Grew up in Dallas and was once a cheerleader as well as an actor. He went on to produce top rated TV series such as *Charlie's Angels, Melrose Place, Fantasy Island,* and *Beverly Hills 90210,* to name a few.

♦ JERRY HALL: Native of Mesquite, Texas; retired cheerleader, actress, supermodel, musician, and Mick Jagger's ex.

- **KAY BAILEY HUTCHINSON:** U.S. senator from Texas and former UT cheerleader.

- **SISSY SPACEK:** Majorette in Quitman, Texas, actress and movie star.

FAMOUS INVENTIONS FROM TEXAS (OR BY TEXANS)

• The Dr Pepper Company is the oldest major manufacturer of soft drink concentrates and syrups in the United States. It was created, manufactured, and sold beginning in 1885 in the Central Texas town of Waco. Dr Pepper is a "native Texan," originating at Morrison's Old Corner Drug Store. It is the oldest of the major brand soft drinks in America. Charles Alderton, a young pharmacist working at Morrison's store, is believed to be the inventor of the now famous drink.

• Liquid Paper correction fluid was invented by former Monkee Michael Nesmith's mother. Bette Nesmith Graham came up with the idea of using a small bottle

she improved the formula, changed its name to Liquid Paper, and set out to trademark the name and
patent her product. After IBM passed on her offer to
sell Liquid Paper to them, Bette started marketing
the product on her own. Liquid Paper, Inc., did not
become profitable for several years, and it was not
until the mid-1960s that Liquid Paper correction
fluid began to generate substantial income for its inventor. Liquid Paper was sold to the Gillette Corpo-
ration in 1979 for $47.5 million (plus a royalty on
every bottle sold until the year 2000). Bette Nesmith
Graham died in 1980, leaving half her fortune to her
son Michael, and half to philanthropic organizations.

◆ The all-American meal, the hamburger, was created
in Athens, Texas.

◆ Charles Goodnight is credited with inventing the
chuckwagon (a cowboy's portable kitchen wagon,
used on the cattle trails) in 1866.

◆ The Ruby Red Grapefruit was invented by A. E. Hen-
niger in Weslaco, Texas, in 1929.

◆ The heart Pacemaker was invented by Otis Boykin,
born in 1920 in Dallas; his death was pretty ironic,

because it could have been prevented by this, his most famous invention.

- Henry Garrett invented the first car radio in the early 1920s and possibly the first automatic electric traffic light.

- The first integrated circuit, which became the microchip, was invented by Jack Kilby in 1958 at Texas Instruments.

- The idea for the ATM machine came from Don Wetzel in the 1960s.

- The frozen margarita was invented by Dallas restaurateur Mariano Martinez in 1971.

- Inspired by his daughter's Super Ball, Dallas's Lamar Hunt, owner of the Kansas City Chiefs, coined "Super Bowl."

ONLY IN TEXAS

———◆———

- Texas is the only state that permits residents to cast absentee ballots from space (thanks to NASA in Houston).

- The Constitution of 1845, which was the resolution that allowed Texas into the Union, stated that Texas had the right to divide into four states in addition to the original Texas. That legal right still remains true.

- To be elected in the State of Texas, one must believe in a supreme being.

- The Texas Rangers form the oldest law-enforcement agency in North America with statewide jurisdiction. They often have been compared to four other world-famous agencies: the FBI, Scotland Yard, Interpol, and the Royal Canadian Mounted Police.

- President Sam Houston (Republic of Texas) was the only foreign leader to serve in the U.S. Senate.

- The State Capitol in Austin is the nation's largest statehouse, with a dome seven feet taller than that of the National Capitol in Washington, D.C.

- A pecan tree is planted in soil from all the 254 Texas counties and stands on the west side of the north entrance of the State Capitol at Austin. The celebrated tree was planted on May 30, 1945, in memory of the Texans who died in World War II.

- Texas is the only state to have had the flags of six different nations fly over it. They are: Spain, France, Mexico, Republic of Texas, Confederate States, and the United States.

- In Texas, filibuster rules are very strict. During the filibuster, the speaker may not eat, though candies and throat lozenges are allowed. There are no bathroom privileges, but astronaut relief kits may be used. No leaning on the desk for support is tolerated, and the speaker's voice must be audible.

- Texas is 801 miles wide, from the northwest corner of the Panhandle to the southern tip of the state, and 773 miles long from the western tip near El Paso to the Sabine River, the easternmost boundary of the state.

◆ Texas is the only state to enter the United States by treaty, instead of territorial annexation.

◆ Marble Falls, Texas, is the only U.S. town laid out by a blind man. General Adam R. Johnson had traveled extensively over this area before he was blinded in the Civil War. From memory, he plotted and surveyed the site for the town in 1886. He was aided by a black man, Earl Moore, who acted as his eyes.

———•———

THE SHOW
THAT WASN'T

For almost thirty years *Austin City Limits* and I have interacted much in the same manner of Joseph Heller's fabled covenant with God: we've left each other alone. There's a reason for this. In all its storied, glorified history as the longest-running music show on television, *ACL* has taped only one performance that it has steadfastly refused to air: mine. I'm not bitter about this, though I am bitter about almost everything else. Indeed, I take a somewhat perverse pride in the fact that, way back in 1976, Kinky Friedman and the Texas Jewboys were considered too risky, too controversial, and very possibly, too downright repellent for public television. For years my performance could be seen only at the Jim Morrison Museum in Waco, but now that Janet Jackson has bared herself to the world, it's time for me to make a clean breast of things as well.

For a while after the show didn't air, I was in a mild snit. In fact, I contemplated committing suicide by jumping through a ceiling fan. Fortunately, I'm of average height, so the ceiling fan would have merely provided me with a mullet, which definitely wasn't in at the time. If I'd been as tall as Ray Benson, of Asleep at the Wheel—the world's tallest living Jew—I might have actually croaked myself. Ray, it should be noted, is not a suicide risk, having been on *ACL* about 117 times. Over the years, in fact, just about everybody in the musical universe has been on the show, with the possible exception of the great Buddy Rich. When Buddy was at last preparing to spring from his mortal coil, a nurse in his hospital room asked him if there was anything that was making him uncomfortable. "Yes," he told her. "Country music." That was probably why they didn't have Buddy on the show.

> I contemplated committing suicide by jumping through a ceiling fan.

There have been other great artists whom the powers that be have deemed not ready for prime time. Years before *ACL* gave the Kinkster the old heave-ho, George D. Hay threw Elvis Presley off the Grand Ole Opry and told him to go back to driving a truck. Elvis is said to have cried on that occasion. He left Nashville, but he didn't remain a trucker for long. Some years later, when he was an international superstar, he happened to be at a party in Music City, when a record company flack introduced him to George Hay. Matter-of-factly,

"This town ain't accessible enough for both of us!"

without malice, Elvis shook hands with him and said, "I know you. You're the man who made me cry."

Watching a bootleg video of my non-show recently was almost enough to make me cry. It was a bit like a funeral or a high school reunion, events that register faithfully the rapid and ruthless passage of time. There I was in the spotlight, wearing an Indian headdress, big blue aviator glasses, a furry blue guitar strap, and a sequined pair of bell-bottom trousers— and this was almost thirty years before *Queer Eye for the Straight Guy*. The headdress had gotten me into trouble before, during a show in that most-liberated of all places, San Francisco, when Buffy Sainte-Marie chased me around the stage attempting to snatch the offending warbonnet off my head. She did not succeed, but the two of us hopped around in an angry circle for about five minutes to the delight of the crowd.

As I watched the ancient concert, I didn't get that dated, insects-trapped-in-amber feeling I often have when watching *Leave It to Beaver* reruns. If the clothing and some of the hairstyles were clearly from another time warp, the social satire seemed to be more applicable to 2005 than to 1976. What the hell; every great artist should always be ahead of his time and behind on his rent. As Bob Dylan has said, art should not reflect a culture; it should subvert it.

There certainly seemed to be plenty of that going on in the video. There was, for instance, our song about the Statue of Liberty, "Carryin' the Torch," in which our drummer, Major Boles, played the last chorus using American flags for drumsticks. And who could forget "They Ain't Makin' Jews Like Jesus Anymore," which contained a line that even Mel Gibson could get behind: "We Jews believe it was Santa Claus who killed Jesus Christ." There was also a spirited version of "Proud to Be an Asshole From El Paso," which stated emphatically: "God and Lone Star beer are things we trust" and "The wetbacks still get twenty cents an hour." And there was the ballad "Rapid City, South Dakota," which was recorded by Dwight Yoakam twenty-five years later—the first country song to touch on the subject of abortion.

> Elvis shook hands with him and said, "I know you. You're the man who made me cry."

I don't like to put myself up on a pedestal, but the concert was pretty damn good. I wish you could've seen it. On the other hand, all of life is perception. George Bernard Shaw was such a genius that he could review a play without even seeing it. As Sherlock Holmes once said, "What you do in this world is a matter of no consequence. The question is, What can you make people believe that you have done?"

In any case, when the producers of *ACL,* in their infinite wisdom, decided not to air the show, the legend only grew. Had they gone ahead and run it, I'd undoubtedly be playing a beer joint tonight on the backside of Buttocks, Texas. I'd never have had the chance to become a best-selling novelist, a friend of presidents, and a candidate for governor. So, God bless *Austin City Limits.*

Today I have many fans, not all of whom are attached to the ceiling. They listen to the songs that made me infamous and read the books that made me respectable. To some, I'm a Renaissance Texan. To others, I'm just another asshole from El Paso wearing a cowboy hat and smoking a cigar. Take, for instance, the manager of a Barnes and Noble in New York.

> Every great artist should always be ahead of his time and behind on his rent.

When the publicist for my recent novel, *The Prisoner of Vandam Street,* told him that I'd be there in person to give a reading, the manager was impressed. "Oh, great!" he said. "Is Kinky going to be wearing his costume?"

THE REDHEADED
STRANGER

———————•———————

It's a rainy January night in 1990 in Austin, Texas, and
Willie's bus is parked near the set of *Another Pair of Aces,*
a movie he's starring in with Kris Kristofferson and Rip Torn.
I climb aboard the bus and find Willie dressed in a flashy sport
jacket, slacks, shiny new boots, and a big, black cowboy hat.

"I hope these are from wardrobe," I say.

Willie smiles and nods. "As you've probably noticed,"
Willie says, "I'm homeless and penniless and now residing
with Little Joe and his family in Temple, Texas. I've been
callin' around lookin' for one of those suicide machines. I'll go
on national TV, hook myself up to that machine, and tell
everyone I have 'til seven o'clock to get sixteen million dollars. If I don't get it, I'm pulling the plug. Just like that guy
Oral Roberts did. And he's still around."

"What's it like to owe this much money?" I ask.

"I started out thinking if I ever got fifty thousand dollars in debt, I'd be a pretty successful cowboy," says Willie. "Considering how far in debt I am now, I'm really cuttin' a big hog in the ass."

Willie wants it known that he is not a tax dodger. Since 1983, he has paid more than eight million dollars in taxes, and his records are up-to-date and current. The problem, according to Willie, was listening to bad advice about a tax-shelter scheme. Willie, who has dedicated so much of his time and efforts to helping others, does not really want to accept Willie Aid. He suggests that if people want to help, they should buy his album *The IRS Tapes,* which consists of unreleased material confiscated from his recording studio before it was locked

up by the IRS. Willie has met with the IRS, and the people there seem to like the idea, too. Soon Willie plans to be on the road again.

There is in Willie a spirit of calm, upbeat determination, in a situation many would regard as hopeless, tragic, or impossible. He is a man behind a sixteen-million-dollar eight ball, but like a timeless spiritual hustler, Willie Nelson is chalking his cue.

"According to the *National Enquirer*," I say, "you're gonna have a hell of a time singing your way back from a debt that large."

Willie's eyes shine. "Watch me," he says.

Both of us laugh. My thoughts wander back to an earlier time, five months and sixteen million dollars ago . . .

It's a Bloody Mary morning, 4:45 A.M. I'm loitering in the parking lot of a convenience store on the outskirts of Tedious, Texas, watching a large Hispanic male projectile vomiting on the only pay phone in the place. Not an auspicious beginning. At five o'clock, I'm supposed to call Doug Holloway, my contact man. The mission: To travel across America on the bus with Willie Nelson and attempt to cajole a hip, quirky profile that shows a side of the star no American has ever seen with the naked eye.

I make the call.

By dawn's surly light, I'm aboard Willie's beautiful touring bus, the only other two occupants being Willie's driver, Gates "Gator" Moore, and Ben Dorsey, who at sixty-five is said to be the world's oldest roadie, having worked for every major country star in the firmament, including a long stint as John Wayne's valet. I mention that being Willie's valet must be easier since the only accouterments he employs are a pair of tennis shoes and a bandanna that has been carbon-dated and found to be slightly older than the shroud of Turin. Dorsey does not respond. The bus lurches onto the highway.

We stop to pick up Willie's sister, Bobbie Nelson, keyboard player for the band. She is a charming and gracious lady, and she likes men who smoke cigars on buses. Bobbie has known Willie longer than anyone on the planet. "He was my little brother," she says. "Now he's my big brother."

I think about my own relationship with Willie. He and I have been friends for a long time, and one of the secrets of our enduring friendship is that we've usually stayed the hell away from each other. I do not want to trick the prey, but I do want to catch him. The situation is somewhat uncomfortable and reminds me of Oscar Wilde's description of a fox hunt: "The unspeakable in pursuit of the inedible."

> One of the secrets of our enduring friendship is that we've usually stayed the hell away from each other.

We pick up the man who was once Bobbie Nelson's little brother in Abbot, Texas, the place where he was born and now lives with his new love, Annie, their two infant children, and their two Mexican nannies, whose only word of English appears to be *Weeeellie*! I do not bring up Willie's problems with the IRS, but Willie does. It seems Willie owes the IRS more millions than there are cross ties on the railroad or stars in the sky. Sister Bobbie is very concerned. "I don't know what people with minds of machinery will do," she says. "Willie's worked so long and hard for this, and now he could lose everything."

Willie himself does not say much about this possibility. The case is current, and he's countersuing. There is a lot of money involved. Willie plays over two hundred dates a year and earns roughly fifty thousand dollars per gig.

As the bus roars toward Texarkana on the way to Detroit, we talk about the situation. Willie, relaxed and philosophical, is not the kind of man who would be likely to jump out the window of his bus.

"You're a gypsy, Willie," I say. "And a gypsy's definition of a millionaire is not a man who has a million dollars, but a man who's spent a million dollars."

Willie laughs as we sit at the little table on the bus. His eyes look into me with all the even-mindedness of a mahatma. "It's like this," Willie says. "I have the ability to make money. I have the ability to owe money. I have the ability to spend money. And I'm proud of it. I'm the perfect American."

> A gypsy's definition of a millionaire is not a man who has a million dollars, but a man who's spent a million dollars.

I ask Willie about the woman who's garnered some press lately in the tabloids with a rather unusual story. She claims that on January 4, 1985, in the Biloxi, Mississippi, Hilton, she and Willie had sexual intercourse for nine consecutive hours and that he consummated the act with a backward somersault with the woman still attached. She's now suing Willie for fifty million dollars for breach of promise in refusing to marry her. At Willie's Fourth of July picnic in Austin, he told me that this was the only true story ever written about him. Now he seems to hedge a bit.

"I'm not saying it didn't happen," he says. "It might've happened. But you would've thought I'd remember at least the first four or five hours."

"What will you do," I ask him, "if the case actually comes to court?"

Willie thinks for a moment, then smiles. "My ex-wife Shirley said she'd be glad to testify on my behalf," he says.

The bus moves like a patient brush stroke across the sepia Arkansas twilight. Inside, as peaceful as a still-life painting, Willie sits across the little table, the conversation moving into the murky casino of world politics.

"You've got to look for the good in everything," says Willie. "Desert Storm took the heat off Roseanne Barr and Neil Bush."

Willie has no great empathy for Neil Bush, but he does feel something for Roseanne Barr. "I can sympathize with anyone who has to sing that song," he says.

> "The teleprompter wasn't rolling at the same speed that I was."
> —WILLIE NELSON

Willie belongs to that small, close-knit fraternity—consisting primarily of Robert Goulet, Pia Zadora, Roseanne Barr, and himself—who have botched the singing of "The

Star-Spangled Banner." At the 1980 Democratic Convention, Willie accidentally blew the chorus, leaving out the entire portion beginning with "And the rocket's red glare . . ." and ending the song quite a bit earlier than expected. Democrats, putting the best face on it, maintained that Willie had deliberately deleted the violence from the song, the "bombs bursting in air," etcetera. Republicans, not being so charitable, contended that Willie was bombed himself at the time. Today Willie merely says: "The teleprompter wasn't rolling at the same speed that I was."

Around midnight a storm comes up, and we see lightning lashing the Nashville skyline almost as if God is smiting the Philistines, who never understood Willie Nelson. In the song "Me and Paul," Willie acknowledges that "Nashville was the roughest," but tonight he seems to hold little rancor for the town that once drove him to lie down in the middle of snowy Broadway and wait for a truck to run him over.

"As they go," I say, "that was a fairly ballsy suicide attempt."

"At three o'clock in the morning in Nashville," says Willie, "there's not that much traffic."

As we roar through Music City, its bright lights and dark shadows do not appear to evoke any bitter memories in Willie. Ben Dorsey, the world's oldest roadie, has joined in the conversation, which has now turned to bandannas, John Wayne, and the Trilateral Commission. Willie is a believer in bandannas and the Trilateral Commission, but he isn't sure about John Wayne.

"I'm a Gene Autry/Roy Rogers guy," Willie says. "John Wayne couldn't sing, and his horse was never smart."

This kind of loose talk irks Dorsey, who, of course, was the Duke's valet for many years before he worked for Willie. Dorsey staunchly defends Wayne and relates a few narratives about beautiful women, freight elevators, seven-passenger roadsters, and Tijuana, at the end of which Willie concedes to Dorsey that Wayne was indeed a great American. I inquire if it's true, as Nashville's famous Captain Midnite asserts, that Willie stole the idea of wearing the bandanna from Midnite and John Wayne. Willie contends that the bandannas and tennis shoes are not an affectation—they are the outfit he wore as a child, predating Wayne's or Midnite's use of the bandanna. Dorsey takes out a John Wayne book and authenticates that the Duke wore a bandanna in a movie in 1928, five years before Willie was born. The conversation has become metaphysical. "Do you ever think of becoming old?" I ask.

> "John Wayne couldn't sing, and his horse was never smart."
> —WILLIE NELSON
>
> ◆
>
> "I was old before it was fashionable."
> —WILLIE NELSON

"I was old before it was fashionable," Willie says.

We stop at a truck stop on the other side of Nashville to pick up guitar genius Grady Martin. Everyone gets off the bus to eat except Willie, who usually stays on, subsisting almost entirely on fried-egg sandwiches to go and bee pollen. In the early hours of the morning, during the long haul to Detroit, Willie speaks forth on one of his favorite causes: the American farmer.

"Russia's giving its land back to its farmers," Willie says, "and here we're taking it away." The Russians, apparently, have asked Willie to speak to the Russian farmers about trusting their government, something the Russian people haven't given serious thought to in over seventy years. "I don't know how I can tell the Russians to trust their government," he says, "when I don't even trust my own."

I try a few units of bee pollen myself. The conversation has somehow come back to the Trilateral Commission, which, Willie believes, controls the world. This notion is often a favorite of old right-wingers, but looking at Willie, one can't help seeing the man has a far closer spiritual kinship to Che Guevara than to Robert Bork. As I move toward my book, Willie is contending that there were men more powerful than George Bush the elder who are calling the shots. Willie's driver, Gator, shouts back from the front of the bus: "Anybody who can get his old lady's picture on a dollar bill is powerful enough for me."

That night I have a vague, troubling dream of Barbara Bush having sexual intercourse with George Washington and, at the end, performing a backward somersault. I write it off to the bee pollen.

When I wake up it is morning and we're in Detroit. Everyone's already checked into the hotel except Willie and myself. I pour some coffee and peek around the curtains to find that the bus is parked right next to a green lawn with a canopy and many nice, respectable-looking suburban couples having brunch. Willie pulls the curtain back ever so slightly and peers out at the scene like a storybook princess in a tower. He can never be one of these people, and I realize his gypsy lifestyle, his incredible celebrity, and his standard wardrobe all mitigate against it. But if he's a prisoner, I figure, I may as well interrogate.

"How many songs have you written?" I ask him.

"About a thousand," Willie says.

"How many kids do you have?

"About a thousand."

"How many wives have you had?"

"Four."

"How many albums have you made?"

"Over a hundred."

"How many cars have you wrecked?"

"Over a hundred."

"Ever been really brokenhearted?"

"I've had a trail of broken hearts," he says. "At the Hank Williams level."

"Doesn't part of you dream of being one of those people out there?" I ask a bit rhetorically. "Of having a little house with a white picket fence and polishing your car under the airport flight path?"

Willie doesn't answer me directly. Maybe there is no direct answer. "I had to stop thinking that I had a home," he says. "You've got to be able to move to the next big town without slashing your wrists."

"At least it must be comforting," I say, "to realize that your ex-wives and ex-girlfriends have to listen to your music in elevators and dentist's waiting rooms."

Willie laughs. "The one nice thing about all my marriages," he says, "is that every time I start a new relationship, all my old lines are good again."

"What effect does marijuana have on you?"

"It makes the questions further apart," he says, "but my answers are still wise and heavy." I see that Willie is again toying, rather poignantly it seems, with the curtain at the window. "If you couldn't sing or write or play the guitar," I ask, "what do you think you would've been?"

Willie steals another shy glance at the nice people eating their mushroom quiches. "A lawyer slash pimp," he says.

"I'm not sure that we really need the slash," I say.

The show at the Michigan State Fair that night is so vibrant, spirited, and full of energy one might not believe every member in the seven-piece band, except Mickey Raphael and Bee Spears, is over fifty. Maybe they're all on bee pollen. The large crowd, seemingly as diverse as America itself, is warm and enthusiastic toward Willie—almost as if he were a personal friend. There are surprisingly large numbers of blind people, adults and children in wheelchairs, and one ambulance with the back doors open and a frail old lady lying inside. The next day I'm having a drink in the hotel bar with Larry Trader, Willie's old pal and promoter and the man who once helped my former band the Texas Jewboys escape a redneck lynch mob in Nacogdoches, Texas. I mention to Trader about the wheelchairs, the blind people, the lady in the ambulance.

"I ain't sayin' he's a doctor," Trader says. "I'm sayin' he's a healer through music."

On the road to New York and Vermont, in Columbo-like fashion, I ask penetrating questions and occasionally get fairly wiggy answers that I write down in my special investigator's notebook. At the Holiday Inn pool in Syracuse, New York, I ask Mickey Raphael, Willie's harmonica player, how it feels to be the only person of the Jewish persuasion in Willie's outfit.

"Fine," says Raphael, "but playing harp with Willie, manipulating the media, and controlling world banking is really wearing me out."

Backstage, I talk to Paul English, Willie's drummer, after the show at the New York State Fair. I ask him what he thinks of the woman who claims she had a "nine-hour nonstop love-a-thon" with the Redheaded Stranger.

"Well," says English, "at least she got her fifty million dollars' worth."

Willie's daughter Lana also has a comment about the rather unusual, not to say sordid, affair. "If Mama were alive right now," says Lana, "I know she'd be wondering whatever happened to her other eight and a half hours."

On the large patio of a Vermont luxury hotel with a vaguely mental-hospital ambience, Jody Payne, Willie's guitar player, is telling me how he first met Willie. It was 1962, and Willie had sat in for a few songs at the West Fort Tavern in Detroit, where Payne was working. Willie sang "Half a Man," and the brilliance of the song completely blew Payne away. Then the owner of the bar came over to Payne and said: "Don't let him sing anymore. He's the worst singer I've ever heard in my life."

Willie was playing bass for Ray Price at the time. "It took Ray almost six months to realize Willie couldn't play bass," says Payne. "It took us about five minutes."

After the show at the Champlain Valley Fair, in Vermont, the bus appears to be surrounded by farmers, Hell's Angels, and American Indians. Willie is taking a break before going out to sign autographs when he suddenly realizes that he is sitting at the table with his longtime manager Mark Rothbaum and Mickey Raphael. Seizing the creative opportunities of the moment, Willie works out a spontaneous improvisation on his song "Why Do I Have to Choose?" He opens his palms in a somewhat Christ-like manner toward Rothbaum and Raphael. Willie sings: "Why Do I Have Two Jews?"

When Willie goes outside again to meet his fans, I take the chance to wander around the backstage area at the fairgrounds. L. G., a Hell's Angel in good standing, is coordinating events with various members of the crew. Gator is organizing routes with the drivers of the three other buses in the entourage, one of which belongs to Shelby Lynne, a young female singer who's opening for Willie and who has one of the most undecaffeinated voices I've ever heard this side of Janis Joplin. Poodie, who first met Willie on the gangplank of Noah's ark, is overseeing the removal of tons of equipment from the stage. Willie's family is packing up to go back on the road. They're a ragged, eccentric, efficient crew, who look for all the world like a band of gypsies who've broken into a Rolex distributorship.

As the fairgrounds empty, I am left with afterimages. I remember walking far into the crowd as Willie sang "Georgia on My Mind," evoking the spirits of Hoagy Carmichael and Richard Manuel. I remember every person in the back of the huge fairgrounds seemingly listening to every word and every note. "Angel Flying Too Close to the Ground." The metal spokes of the wheelchairs. The pulsating neon spokes of the giant Ferris wheel in the nearby field, a world away. Childhood is close by, but you can't quite touch it. "Blue Eyes Cryin' in the Rain." Sister Bobbie playing "Down Yonder" in a style that seems to flutter bravely like a balloon, escaping to some beautiful place between a little country church and an old New Orleans whorehouse. "Just another scene from the world of broken dreams / The night life ain't no good life, but it's my life."

> "Ninety-nine percent of those people are not with their true first choice. That's why they play the jukebox."
> —WILLIE NELSON

I remember walking along the back of the fairgrounds listening to Willie sing, standing in the throng, thinking the thoughts of a lifetime. "You Were Always on My Mind." Willie's voice is not what is traditionally considered a good voice, but it is a great voice and one that is capable of making you cry and comforting you at the same time. It does both to me. I feel a palpable sense of history passing, ephemeral as the dopplered voices on a midway ride, and yet, I know something will stay.

Earlier, backstage, Willie looked out at the crowd. "That's where the real show is," he said. "Ninety-nine percent of those people are not with their true first choice." Willie smiled. Then he added, almost to himself: "That's why they play the jukebox."

As we slowly pull out of the fairgrounds, the curtain is open a bit, and Willie is looking out the window of the bus. Standing behind him, I catch the face of a young girl who suddenly sees him. Her face reflects first disbelief, then a sort of gentle reverence, then the absolute innocence of wonder. Bobbie Nelson's little brother smiles at the girl. The scenery changes. I get back to my notebook, and I realize that there are some things Willie Nelson has that the IRS can never take away.

PART V

LOTTIE'S LOVE

SCOUT'S HONOR

———•———

The first time I went to a charity car wash, Richard Nixon was president. I think some high school cheerleaders were trying to raise money to go to a cheerleading camp in Fat Chance, Arkansas. My vehicle was a dusty green 1953 Plymouth Cranbrook convertible with a wolf whistle and a Bermuda bell. I was hoping to have an overnight with a few of the cheerleaders myself. Of course, that never happened. Nixon would not have approved. Besides, I was a late-blooming serious.

There were a great many things back then, no doubt, of which Nixon and society in general would not have approved. But life was different in those days—or maybe it was exactly the same, only we didn't know it. It seemed, for instance, that none of my high school friends came from broken homes. Divorce was almost unheard of. Nobody knew what a single parent was. And, certainly, I didn't know anyone who had a parent in prison. I don't really think I was sheltered. I just think I was out to lunch.

The first time I went to a charity car wash, Richard Nixon was president.

The second charity car wash of my life was held recently in the parking lot of the Hotel San José in Austin. I was driving a silver 1999 Cadillac DeVille that had once belonged to my father and had the distinction of being one of the few Cadillacs in Texas with a Darwin fish emblem. The vehicles had changed, and I had changed. The game had changed, too, in this tale of two car washes. Whether we like it or not, at some indefinable point in time, we all forsake our childhood games and become players in the game of life.

The girls at the second car wash were not high school cheerleaders. For one thing, most of them weren't old enough to be in high school. For another, in their brief lives, there hadn't been a hell of a lot to cheer about. Girl Scout cookie season was over for this particular troop. So were a few other things, like home, family, and childhood. That's because every girl in this troop has or has had a mother in prison. They are Troop 1500, otherwise known as the Enterprising Girl Scouts Beyond Bars, the Austin chapter of a national program that has served more than forty-five girls with incarcerated parents since its inception in 1998.

And they are enterprising. The car wash was a success, with the girls washing, soaping, and spraying fifteen cars, one bike, themselves, and several customers. And many of the

girls are looking confidently to the future. One bright, witty thirteen-year-old, who was raped by an uncle while her mother was in prison for running a drug ring, reads at least one book a week, and when she grows up she wants to be a librarian. A fifteen-year-old, whose mother is serving time for a gang-related murder, wants to be a marine biologist. A fourteen-year-old, whose mother—a heroin addict who stole and forged checks—wants to be a social worker. Judging by how devotedly she helps the younger girls, she may be well on her way. Then there's the pretty twelve-year-old whose mother is serving fifty years for murder. Her stated goals are to be a horseback-riding instructor and to work with the seals at Schlitterbahn, a water park in the Texas Hill Country. There are, to my knowledge, no seals at Schlitterbahn. They may have them, of course, by the time her mother gets out. And then there's the most soulful little nine-year-old in the world. She wears beautiful braids and has never been able to live with her mother, who's in for the usual things—prostitution, theft, and using and selling heroin and crack cocaine. And the kid? When she grows up, she wants to be a veterinarian.

> Whether we like it or not, at some indefinable point in time, we all forsake our childhood games and become players in the game of life.

Are any of them going to get there? You might be surprised. According to Julia Cuba, the program executive of the Lone Star Council, which oversees Girl Scout troops in eighteen counties in Texas and Oklahoma, 96 percent of the girls in Troop 1500 have stayed in school. Ninety-nine percent have avoided teen pregnancy. Ninety-eight percent have kept out of trouble with the legal system. These are remarkable numbers, especially considering that girls whose mothers are in prison are six times as likely as other high-risk groups to end up in prison.

In the United States, there are approximately thirty Girl Scouts Beyond Bars programs, most of them limited to providing only one service: once-a-month visits to the prisons. The Austin chapter, led by Cuba and regularly evaluated by Darlene Grant, of the School of Social Work at the University of Texas at Austin, differs from the others in that it concerns itself with a girl's family, school, and social life and helps guide her mother's reentry into the free world. The program has been so successful, in fact, that the girls are the focus of a

PBS documentary by award-winning filmmakers Ellen Spiro and Karen Bernstein. The girls are filming part of the documentary themselves.

After I dried off from the car wash, I went out to dinner with the girls. They are a smart, free-spirited, fun-loving bunch of kids. I'd never met them before, and from what I know of life, our paths may never cross again. I've always found it interesting how most of us seem to place our energies and efforts behind only those causes that directly affect our own lives or those

> **Most of us were born lucky. . . . Lucky to have someone to provide hills to climb and stars to reach for.**

of our families. In other words, there are better things to do on a beautiful Saturday afternoon than drive a van full of kids out to Gatesville Prison. I was reminded of a lady I once met whose only grandchild had died. She told me, "I used to say, 'This is my grandson, and those are other people's kids.' Now I say, 'Every child is my grandchild.'"

So why did I allow myself to get soaked to the bone at a Girl Scout car wash in the first place? Just lucky, I guess. And lucky is the right word for it. Most of us were born lucky. Lucky to have a home and a family. Lucky to have someone to provide hills to climb and stars to reach for. Lucky, when we fell, to have a catcher waiting in the rye. The girls at the car wash, of course, have known precious little of those things. Outside of Julia and Darlene, all they really have is each other. Maybe it will be enough. I certainly hope so. As we like to say in rock and roll, the kids are all right.

HAIR TODAY . . .

———————◆———————

Why, you might ask, would a person whose name is Kinky want to fly to a spa in Houston for the express purpose of getting his hair straightened? And why, you might also ask, would a person whose last name is Friedman want to have his moss straightened by a Palestinian? These are some of life's more difficult questions, so don't be surprised if the answers turn out to be a bit, well, kinky.

"Farouk Shami is the greatest hairstylist in the world," said my friend John McCall, giving me a little pep talk as we boarded his private jet. "He's taller, of course, when he's standing on his wallet." John has a pretty thick wallet, too. Formerly the Shampoo King from Dripping Springs, he's now known in hair circles, along with Farouk, as "the father of the Chi iron," a hair-straightening device that is racking up sales almost as big as the hula hoop did in its day.

On the short flight to Houston, John talked shop. "Shampoo," he said, "is all about making people feel better about themselves, thereby making them happier, more satisfied human beings." I'd heard his Shampoo 301 lecture before, but I had to admit that I'd never been able to do anything with my hair. That's why I started growing dreadlocks more than a year ago and only recently cut them off. Shortly thereafter, I allowed my friend Ed Wolff to sell my dreads on eBay. Ed informed me that the first one went for seventy-five dollars to some guy in Dallas. Ed has nine left, and he's holding them until my career takes off or I fall through the trapdoor. I'm trying to be as helpful as I can.

> Why would a person whose last name is Friedman want to have his moss straightened by a Palestinian?

Before the dreads, I got my hair cornrowed, which made me look like a rather anemic, extremely short NBA player. Before that, whenever I removed my cowboy hat, my hair remained in sort of a gelatin mold that I often referred to as my "Lyle Lovett starter kit." So, you can see why I might've wanted to get my hair straightened.

A long, white stretch limo, driven by a cheerful Palestinian named Majed, picked us up at Hobby airport and whisked us off to John and Farouk's BioSilk Spa in the Galleria. The BioSilk Spa, I was informed, had been widely recognized as one of the most magnificent spas in the world. This didn't

mean a hell of a lot to a poor cowboy like myself. I'd been in outhouses, whorehouses, and White Houses, but I was proud to say I'd never darkened the door of a spa.

"Your feet are in beautiful condition," said Demeca as she gave me a pedicure.

"So are your hands," said Nina as she simultaneously gave me a manicure.

"That's because he's never worked a day in his life," said John.

The girls had practically dragged me into the sumptuous spa for these treatments, but I had to admit they felt pretty good. Next Lasonda gave me a killer-bee massage, and Tina gave me a facial. What would John Wayne do? I wondered.

"Is all this necessary?" I asked John irritably. "I came here to get my hair straightened with your damn Chi iron."

"You see?" he said to the girls. "He's more relaxed already."

"Where the hell's Farouk?" I shouted. "Throwing a rock at a tank?"

"No, my dear friend," said a suave voice behind me. I turned and saw Farouk wearing a sharply tailored suit, a pair of red boots, and a charming smile. He was walking toward me brandishing a large gleaming implement that vaguely resembled an abortionist's forceps.

"I'm not pro-choice or pro-life," I said. "I'm pro-football."

Moments later I was sitting in a thronelike chair, with Farouk ironing my hair. White wisps of steam actually rose from the top of my head. The ceramic lining on the Chi iron, he explained, was creating negative ions and causing the cuticles of my hairs to lie down and shine. "Whatever your dreams," he said, "they shall be fulfilled."

It wasn't long before we both discovered a basic law of sci-

> Whenever I removed my cowboy hat, my hair remained in sort of a gelatin mold that I often referred to as my "Lyle Lovett starter kit."
>
> ◆
>
> I'd been in outhouses, whorehouses, and White Houses, but I was proud to say I'd never darkened the door of a spa.

ence: Kinky hair covers bald spots; straight hair does not. The scope of the problem soon became obvious, causing Farouk to have to resort to Plan B, a fairly massive comb-over that made me look like Hitler as a used-car salesman.

Farouk tried to put the best spin on things. "It looks different, doesn't it?" he said enthusiastically. "I have such a wonderful job! I wake up excited every morning because all I do is make women look beautiful and they pay me for it." I did not respond immediately. I was too stunned by my image in the mirror. The top of my head looked very much like a beach toy.

Later that evening, in a fashionable suburban neighborhood, John and I and nineteen members of Farouk's extended family attended a sixty-first birthday bash for Farouk at the Kobe Steakhouse. Majed, the driver, told me he was under the impression that the Kobe Steakhouse was owned by Kobe Bryant. Many of the other patrons in the restaurant, possibly observing the St. Louis Arch on top of my head, were under the impression that I was Prince Charles, down here for a fox-hunting trip.

> **Farouk resorted to Plan B, a fairly massive comb-over that made me look like Hitler as a used-car salesman.**

The festivities were also to celebrate the inauguration of a new business enterprise. With Farouk Systems, the BioSilk Spa, a popular hair conditioner called Silk Therapy, the Chi turbo hair dryer, and the Chi iron under their belts, Farouk and John were both already as rich as Croesus. But Farouk and I had cooked up yet another venture. It would be known as

Farouk and Friedman's Olive Oil, and it would be imported from Farouk's family's orchards south of Jerusalem. The orchards had been tended and harvested by Farouk's ancestors, since before the time of Jesus.

"This could be big!" John said. "Everything Farouk touches turns to gold. That is, everything except Kinky's hair."

"L'Chaim!" said Farouk, lifting his glass.

"To Farouk and Friedman's!" I said. "We might just be the last true hope for peace in the Middle East."

UNLIKELY TEXANS

◆ **BARNEY THE PURPLE DINOSAUR (DALLAS):** Standing six feet tall in his purple stockings, Barney stars in the children's TV show *Barney and Friends*. The character got his start in 1987 in direct-sale videos created by Dallas teacher Sheryl Leach. The tapes caught the eye of the Public Broadcasting System, who put *Barney and Friends* on the air in 1992. The big purple dinosaur quickly became a public phenomenon, joining Mr. Rogers and Jim Henson's Muppets as PBS stars. Barney is a Tyrannosaurus Rex; he is often joined by his pals Baby Bop (a baby Triceratops) and her brother B.J. (a Protoceratops). He starred in a 1997 feature film, *Barney's Great Adventure*.

◆ **CONAN THE BARBARIAN:** The popular literary hero was from the prehistoric land of Cimmeria, but his creater was a Texan, so by proxy Conan himself was a Texan, too. Robert E. Howard, born in 1906 in Peaster, Texas, began writing in 1921 and sold his first story to *Weird Tales* magazine when he was eighteen. Howard created fantasy adventures laid in such mythical kingdoms as Atlantis. Conan the Barbarian was his most popular literary hero.

◆ **CHECKERS,** former President Nixon's black cocker spaniel from Texas saved Nixon's political career in 1952—and by extension caused Watergate. When then-VP candidate Nixon was accused of setting up a secret slush fund, he appeared on television and said, in what came to be known as the "Checkers Speech," the only gift he'd received from his political cronies was Checkers. His children loved that dog, Nixon said, and he wasn't going to give it back—even if it was a crime. America wept. Nixon went on to become vice president under Eisenhower and, of course, later became president.

◆ **JOAN CRAWFORD** (real name: Lucille Fay Leseu): Born in San Antonio, Texas, on March 23, 1906. Early in her film career MGM head Louis B. Mayer launched a fan-magazine contest to find Lucille Leseu a new name. The result was "Joan Crawford," a name she claimed she never liked. Her career with MGM stretched from 1925 to 1942, and she became one of that company's biggest stars. By the late 1930s, Mommie Dearest was one of Hollywood's highest paid actresses. In the late 1950s with her career on the wane, Crawford made a surprising comeback in the highly successful, *What Ever Happened to Baby Jane?* (1962). Her film career spanned more than forty years and included performances in more than eighty films. She made her last movie in 1970.

◆ **VANILLA ICE:** Pre-dated Eminem by a decade as the first "white" rapper to hit the charts with two top-ten albums and a (failed) feature film. He created a controversy when his management was reported to have fabricated his thug background—he wasn't a street kid from the ghetto in Miami, he was a wealthy country club kid from Dallas.

◆ **CYD CHARISSE** (real name: Tula Ellice Finklea) was born in Amarillo, Texas, on March 8, 1921. When she was sixteen, she married a Frenchman named Nico Charisse. They operated a ballet school and later Nico encouraged Cyd to work in feature film ballet numbers. MGM Studios recognized her talent and courted her heavily to appear in their musical. In 1946, she briefly appeared with Fred Astaire in the opening number of producer Arthur Freed's *Zeigfeld Follies*. Her uncredited appearance with Fred Astaire got her a seven-year contract with MGM. She appeared in a number of musicals over the next few years, but it was *Singin' in the Rain* (1952) with Gene Kelly that made her a big star. That was quickly followed by her great performance in *The Band Wagon* (1953). As the 1960s came, musicals faded from the screen, as did her career. She made appearances on television and performed in a nightclub revue with her second husband, singer Tony Martin.

THINGS THAT MAKE YOU GO "WTF?"

- During the 2004 presidential election, John Kerry's hometown newspaper, the *Lowell Sun,* endorsed George W. Bush for president. Bush's hometown newspaper, the *Lone Star Iconoclast,* endorsed John Kerry for president.

- There is a petrified buffalo hairball at the Texas Ranger Hall of Fame in Waco.

- The movie *Paris, Texas* was banned in the city of Paris, Texas, shortly after its box office release.

- Owning a Bowie knife in Texas is illegal.

- College Station, Texas—Honored Dead Mascots: The graves of Reveille the Collie I-V have been moved from their former location outside Kyle Field, Texas A&M, due to construction activity. The new construction will remove the tunnel from which the former mascots used to view the scoreboard. Recently, a Corps of Cadets member has stood near the new gravesite with a dry erase board updating the score for the deceased canines. There has been discussion of making this a permanent tradition.

- Slug Bug Ranch, Conway, Texas: Five Volkswagen Bugs buried nose down in the ground similar to Cadillac Ranch. The site is about eighteen miles east of the eastern edge of Amarillo. It's an open-air display and is accessible twenty-four hours a day at no cost. Directions: Conway, Texas. I-40, exit 96. Right off the Interstate at the southwest corner of the exit. East of Amarillo, Texas, on I-40.

- James H. Turner, a soldier, was sentenced to three years in the penitentiary at Huntsville in 1872 for "worthlessness." He was found by the military to be "totally unfit in deportment and character for a soldier due to general worthlessness and by lying, stealing, drinking intoxicating liquors, and other persistent meanness."

- Toilet Seat Art Museum, Alamo Heights, Texas: Barney Smith is a master in the art of decorating toilet seats, and he's got 616 examples hanging in his garage museum to prove it. His Toilet Seat Art Museum is a real traffic stopper as he swings open the doors, exposing his artistic endeavors for all the world to see. A retired master plumber, Barney, now in his eighties, has been painting "theme" toilet seats as a hobby for thirty-two years. Along with discarded seats, plumbing supply houses send him their damaged seats, and he decorates each one with something special. Each seat is numbered, cataloged, and then documented with information about the materials he used for decoration, who might have donated the materials, and what inspired the idea. His seats display, among other things, a piece of the Berlin Wall, barbed wire from a World War II concentration camp, and a piece of insulation from the *Challenger* space shuttle explosion. Less infamous art includes arrowheads, license plates, Pokemon cards, casket handles, and tributes to all the service clubs in America. Be sure to sign his guest book; he's had visitors from forty-four countries. Toilet Seat Art Museum, 239 Abiso, Alamo Heights, Texas 78209.

- By proclamation of Governor George W. Bush, June 10, 2000, was "Jesus Day" in Texas, a day that "challenges people to follow Christ's example by performing good works in their communities and neighborhoods."

- The Texas legislature once passed a resolution honoring a serial killer. In 1971, Representative Tim Moore Jr. of Waco sponsored a resolution in the Texas House of Representatives in Austin calling on the House to commend Albert de Salvo for his unselfish service to "his country, his state, and his community." The resolution stated that "this compassionate gentleman's dedication and devotion to his work has enabled the weak and the lonely throughout the nation to achieve and maintain a new degree of concern for their future." The resolution passed unanimously. Representative Moore then revealed that he had only tabled the motion to show how the legislature passes bills and resolutions often without reading them or understanding what they say. Albert de Salvo was the Boston Strangler.

MAN ABOUT TOWN

In 1985, after the death of my mother, I left New York for good to seek shelter in the small towns that lay scattered about the Hill Country as if they were peppered by the hand of God onto the gravy of a chicken-fried steak. In New York, people believe that nothing of importance ever happens outside the city, that if it doesn't occur inside their own office, it hasn't occurred at all. My friends told me that I would be a quitter if I gave up whatever the hell I was doing in New York and went back home. One of the things I was doing was large quantities of Peruvian marching powder, and I now believe that leaving may have saved my life.

I'd had, it seemed, seven years of bad luck. One of my two great loves, Kacey Cohen, had kissed a windshield at 95 miles per hour in her Ferrari. My other great love, of course, was me. My best friend, Tom Baker, troublemaker, had overdosed in New York. I'd come back to Austin just in time to spend a few months with my mother before she died. My dear Minnie, from whom much of my soul springs, left me with three cats, a typewriter, and a talking car. She wanted me to be in good company, to write, and to have somebody to talk to. The car's name was Dusty. She was a 1983 Chrysler LeBaron convertible with a large vocabulary, including the phrase, "A door is ajar." At this time of my life, one definitely was. My mother had always believed in me. Now, it seemed, it was time for me to believe in myself.

After New York, you'd think Austin would be a pleasant relief, but to my jangled mind, there still seemed to be too many people. So I corralled Cuddles, Dr. Skat, and Lady into Dusty, and together we drifted up to the Hill Country, where

"Yuppies Kimosabe. Thousands of them."

the people talk slow, the hills embrace you, and the small towns flash by like bright stations reflecting on the windows of a train at night. As Bob Dylan once wrote, "It takes a train to cry." As I once wrote, "Anything worth cryin' can be smiled."

What is it about small towns that always seems to be oddly comforting? Jesus was born in one. James Dean ran away from one. While visiting Italy, my father once said, "If you've seen one Sistine Chapel, you've seen them all." This is true of small towns as well, except they're not particularly good places to get postcards from. "Why would anyone want to live here?" somebody always says. "It's out in the middle of nowhere. It's so far away." And the gypsy answers, "From where?"

> **Dusty was a 1983 Chrysler LeBaron convertible with a large vocabulary, including the phrase, "A door is ajar."**

There is a fundamental difference between big-city and country folks. In the city you can honk at the traffic, shout epithets, and shoot the bird at anybody you like. You know you'll probably never see those people again. In a small town, you're responsible for your behavior. Instead of spouting off, you simply have to smile and shake your head. You know you're going to see the same people again in church or maybe at a cross burning. (Just kidding.)

Another positive aspect of living in or near small towns is that they're breeding grounds for some of the most colorful characters on the planet. They're also good places to hear stories about snakes. Dry cleaning's cheaper than it is in the big city, and life itself perhaps is a bit more precious, always al-lowing for inflation. There is, of course, no dry cleaner's in Medina. You have to go to Bandera. And if you want to rent a good video, you probably should go to Kerrville. I say this because the Bandera video store has *Kiss of the Spider Woman* racked in the section with *Friday the 13th* and *The Texas Chainsaw Massacre*.

Arguably Agatha Christie's greatest creation, Miss Marple, hailed from the small English town of St. Mary Mead. In a lifetime of fictional crime detection, the sage Miss Marple contended that the true character of people anywhere in the world could be easily divined by casting her mind back to the people she'd grown up with. For

> **"If you've seen one Sistine Chapel, you've seen them all."**
> —TOM FRIEDMAN

instance, the shy Peeping Tom in London reminded her keenly of the butcher's son in St. Mary Mead, who'd been slightly off-kilter but would never have harmed a flea. In such manner, she determined that he was not the murderer of the fifth Duchess of Phlegm-on-Rye. In other words, the small town, like the small child, often dictates the emotional heritage of the human race.

So, maybe there's not that much difference between small-town life and life in the big city. When I lived in New York, like most New Yorkers, I rarely ventured outside my own little neighborhood in the Village. I bought newspapers at the same stand every morning, frequented the same cigar shop near Sheridan Square, and hung out at a bar right across the avenue called the Monkey's Paw. Like most Manhattanites, I never went to Brooklyn, never visited the Statue of Liberty, never ascended to the top of the Empire State Building, and never took a ride on the Staten Island Ferry. That was all for the tourists, most of whom, ironically, were from small towns.

> **"Everything comes out in the wash if you use enough Tide."**
> —EARL BUCKELEW

My old, departed friend Earl Buckelew, the unofficial mayor of Medina, always used to say, "Everything comes out in the wash if you use enough Tide." Yet there are tides that run deep in small towns, deep as the sea of humanity, deep as the winding, muddy river of life. There once were two lovers who lived in Medina: Earl's youngest son, John, and his true love, the beautiful Janis. Though still in their teens, it is very possible that they shared a love many of us have forfeited, forgotten, or never known. A love of this kind can sometimes be incandescent in its innocence, reaching far beyond the time and geography of the small town into the secret history of the ages.

In June of 1969, at a country dance under the stars, John and Janis quarreled, as true lovers sometimes will. They drove home separately. On the same night Judy Garland died, Janis was killed in a car wreck. John mourned for her that summer, and in September, he took poison on her grave, joining her in eternity. John and Janis were much like another pair of star-crossed young lovers, the subjects of one of that summer's biggest films. The town was too small for a movie theater, but that year, many believe, *Romeo and Juliet* played in Medina.

IF I RAN THE ZOO

Many of us remember, in that dim and distant corridor of childhood, a book titled *If I Ran the Zoo*. What's that? You don't remember reading it? Okay. Push pause. There once was a zoo that some folks liked to call Texas politics. In this zoo were doves and hawks, bulls and bears, crocodiles and two-legged snakes, and lots and lots and lots of sheep. But the ones who ran the zoo were not really animals. They were people dressed up in elephant and donkey suits who'd lined their pockets long ago and now went around lying to everybody and making all the rules. Even as a child I knew I never wanted to be one of them, a perfunctory, political party hack. This did not stop me, of course, from growing up to be a party animal.

Unless you've been living in a double-wide deer blind, you

know I'm running for governor in 2006. Well, I'm a rather in-
decisive person, so I'm not even entirely sure that I'm running
yet. I have to weigh the impact the race may have on my family. You may be thinking, "The Kinkster doesn't have a family." But that's not quite right, folks: Texas is my family. And I
intend to give Texans a governor who knows how to ride, to
shoot straight, and to tell the truth, a governor as indepen-
dent-thinking and as colorful as the state itself.

By running as an independent, I plan to demonstrate that
even if the governor really doesn't do any heavy lifting, he can
still do some spiritual lifting. There's a place above politics
that has nothing to do with bureaucracy where good things
can get done by an outsider who is in time and in tune with
the music flowing from that old, beautiful instrument: the
voice of the people. Unfortunately, where I come from, that
instrument is an accordion.

Being independent is what Texas is all about. Here, someone running from the outside may, in fact, have more chance
than elsewhere to be taken seriously. In Minnesota, few people took Jesse Ventura seriously until, in the wink of an eye,
he put them in a reverse figure-four leg lock. His confronta-
tional style, however, did not serve him well and he lasted
only one term. He never figured out that wrestling is real and
politics is fixed.

Arnold Schwarzenegger is another story. Even far into his
campaign, he was written off by a good part of the electorate.
Then something happened to change all that. The people of
California sensed that the world was watching. (They were
right. We were watching Scott Peterson.) Now they're talking

about running Arnold for president. Many Texans are taking note, thinking that if they can get rid of politicians in California, maybe we can get rid of Californians in Texas.

So how does an independent candidate get taken seriously, particularly one who believes that humor is one of the best ways of getting to the truth? The truth is, if you don't watch out Guam is going to pass us in funding of public education. Beyond its obsession with shaking down lobbyists, the Texas legislature has proved that it is neither a visionary nor an efficient institution. The Fraternal Order of the Bulimic Moose could probably do a better job. A good spay-and-neuter program may be the answer. As my father always said, "Treat children like adults and adults like children." But for God's sake, whether you have to go around them or over them, let's get something done, even if it means invading Oklahoma so we can move up to number forty-eight in the affordability of health care.

> Even if the governor really doesn't do any heavy lifting, he can still do some spiritual lifting.
>
> ◆
>
> "Treat children like adults and adults like children."
> —TOM FRIEDMAN

Here is where the spiritual lifting comes in. Though the governor of Texas holds a largely ceremonial position, you must be able to inspire people, especially young people, to become more involved in the welfare of our state. As I drive around in my Yom Kippur Clipper—which sports a bumper sticker that reads "My Governor Is a Jewish Cowboy"—I am constantly impressed by the young people I run into, sometimes literally.

Take the fellow I met recently. He was a grocery clerk in Del Rio, and he seemed quite bright. As I was talking to him, a customer walked up and asked for half a head of lettuce. The clerk said he'd have to check with the manager, and he walked to the back of the store. Unnoticed by the clerk, the customer walked back there, too, just in time to hear him say to the manager, "Some asshole wants to buy half a head of lettuce." The clerk, suddenly seeing the customer standing next to him, then turned and said, "But this kind gentleman has offered to buy the other half." Later, the manager, complimenting the clerk on his fast thinking, told him that a large Canadian chain was buying the store, and suggested he might climb the ladder quickly. "Everyone in Canada," responded the clerk, "is either a hooker or a hockey player."

"Just a minute, young man," said the manager. "My wife is from Canada."

"No kiddin'," said the clerk. "Who's she play for?"

Young people like this, I believe, can be an inspiration to us all. When I'm governor, many of them will be running the place. And no doubt I'll be running after many of them. Everyone knows we're not going to get any action or inspiration from career politicians. They're so busy holding on to their power they never have time to send the elevator back down.

I'm not afraid to stand for something. I have less political experience than any of them but I'm not worried. Trust me, I'm a Jew. I'll hire good people.

And speaking of good people, lots of them are hitching a ride aboard the ol' Yom Kippur Clipper these days to help with the campaign and be a part of the Friedman administration. George W., who promised to help with my efforts and be my "one-man focus group," is still staying the course. Laura, to whom I'd sent some bumper stickers, expressed her feelings thusly in a recent letter: "The bumper stickers suggest that you've reached a new level of political correctness, even lower than your previous record!" Bill Clinton appears likely to be getting into the act as well. These people, of course, along with many others, are all FOKs. That means, as you no doubt know, Friends of Kinky.

As for Willie Nelson, the Hillbilly Dalai Lama, I'm proud to say he's been a strong supporter of my political ambitions right from the start. When I saw him recently I put it straight to him. "Willie," I said, "when I'm governor is there something more you'd like to do for the people of Texas or do you still just want to be head of the Texas Rangers?" "Let's start with that," he said.

So, do I have a chance to win? Farouk Shami thinks so. He's my Palestinian hairdresser. That's why I always wear a hat. Farouk and Friedman's Olive Oil from the Holy Land, which benefits Israeli and Palestinian children affected by the conflict, is now on the market. When I'm governor, Farouk will be Texas's ambassador to Israel. Little Jewford, the only surviving member of the Texas Jewboys who's still ambulatory, is also highly gratified

> Trust me, I'm a Jew. I'll hire good people.
>
> ◆
>
> "The bumper stickers suggest that you've reached a new level of political correctness, even lower than your previous record!"
> —LAURA BUSH

about being on the short list for first lady. Billy Joe Shaver is prepared to be crowned poet laureate of Texas. And last but not least, the Friedmans, my five dogs, are positively thrilled at embarking (get it?) upon the long and exciting journey to the governor's mansion.

If the petition drive to get on the ballot in March 2006 is successful, I will become the first independent candidate to run for governor since they dragged a heavily monstered Sam Houston out from under the bridge. At the very least, I plan to give people a chance to vote for, rather than against, somebody. And what of the ribbon-cutters? They see the governorship as a comfortable job. I see it as an opportunity to make that Lone Star shine again.

But then, of course, there's always politics as usual. I was showing a friend around Austin recently and he was very impressed with what he saw. "That's a beautiful statue of Governor Rick Perry you all put up," he said.

"That *is* Rick Perry," I said.

START TALKIN': A GUIDE TO KINKYBONICS

Agro American: An Aggie (anyone who attends or has attended Texas A&M University in College Station, Texas).

the Anti-Hank: Originally meant to refer to Garth Brooks, but has expanded to include any boring, meaningless, mainstream country singer.

Au'un: Pronounced "AW-nnn." Refers to Austin, Texas.

A big hairy: A large steak.

Bugled to Jesus: To die. (On loan from Larry L. King.) *See also* Step on a rainbow.

Bull fuck against a barn door: A term of endearment intended to convey "I find you appealing and would like to get to know you better."

Crumpet-chomping Neville Chamberlain surrender monkey: Refers to British people. Often shortened to "crumpet chomper."

Dallet: Dallas, Texas.

Dr. Pecker: Dr Pepper, a soda invented in Waco, Texas.

Financial pleasure: Something worth doing.

George Bush's rabbi: Kinky's self-appointed position in the Bush administration.

to Get Starbucked into the twenty-first century: Describes a once cool individual who has sold out and become just another part of the herd killing time at Starbucks while sipping a skinny latte and reading the *Wall Street Gerbil*.

Hand me my thunderstick: Give me another cigar.

to Hose: 1) To have sexual intercourse; 2) To get cheated.

Hootball: Pronounced like "football" but with an "h" and a strong emphasis on the first syllable. "I'm gonna watch some HOOTball."

Hoss: Used interchangably with "pal" and "brother." Something you say to a male friend in lieu of using his name. Example: "For God's sake, hoss! You can't put George Bush's rabbi in a mental hospital!"

I'm going to commit suicide by jumping through a ceiling fan: Expresses Kinky's dissatisfaction with a current situation. Related to "I'm going to kill myself in honor of your visit to Texas."

Jesus boots: Sandals.

Jew canoe: A Cadillac car. *See also* Yom Kippur Clipper.

Kerrvert: A resident of Kerrville, Texas.

Killer bee: Excellent; very, very good. Example: "Lasonda gave me a killer-bee massage."

Kinkster: Kinky's term of endearment for himself.

Lyle Lovett starter kit: Kinky's description of his own hair.

May the good Lord take a likin' to ya: Said as a parting gesture. (On Loan from Roy Rogers.)

the Medina wave: A driver encountering another vehicle on the highway will casually, effortlessly raise his index finger from the wheel in a brief salute, acknowledging the other driver, the countryside, and life in general. The other driver, unless he's new to these parts (the Texas Hill Country), will respond in kind.

Moss: Hair.

Nutshell it: Get to the point. *See also* Put it on a bumper sticker.

Okay you guys . . . : Means it's time for you to leave because your presence is starting to irritate the Kinkster. Don't make him say it more than once.

Pardon me!: Said in a falsetto voice after an interminable belch done in polite company, usually in a restaurant. Can be accompanied by pretending the coffee cup said it.

Peruvian marching powder: Cocaine.

Pony up some bucks: Contribute money.

Power nap: A very brief nap.

Put a sock in it: Shut the fuck up.

Put it on a bumper sticker: Get to the point. *See also* Nutshell it.

Resign from the human race: To take a sabbatical.

Rocket beans: Amphetamines. Kinky took enormous quantities of rocket beans to get through the trauma of attending the University of Texas and ended up staying awake for five years in a row in Nashville, Tennessee.

Slit: A woman. Not intended to be pejorative.

a Snit: To be angry or irritated at someone. Example: "You're not still in a snit about that whole belching the Lord's Prayer thing I did at Luby's yesterday, are you?"

Start talkin': The phone rings. Pick it up and snarl, "Start talkin'!" instead of a pleasant "Hello?" like everyone else.

Step on a rainbow: To die. *See also* Bugled to Jesus.

Stick a fork in your eye: A phrase indicating displeasure; related to "commiting suicide by jumping through a ceiling fan."

Sugar on his/her face: The white fur on an elderly dog's muzzle.

Take a Nixon: To take a shit. If you really want to be like Kinky, you would be able to complete the entire process of taking a Nixon in two minutes or under, including announcing the impending Nixon, getting up and walking to the bathroom, completing the act, washing your hands, and strolling back to the table while belching, "I like it here!"

Tennis shoe the bill: To skip out on an unpaid bill.

Water your lizard: To urinate, preferably outdoors.

Tedious: A stand-alone statement used to describe a person, situation, idea, etc. Example: "Kinky, did you see that precious little boy in the tiny cowboy boots?"—"Tedious."

Uton: Pronounced "UTE-un." Refers to Houston, Texas.

Waitret: A waitress.

Waldheimer's Disease: An infliction that prevents a person from remembering he or she was once a Nazi. Named after Kurt Waldheim, former secretary of the United Nations, who was outed as a Nazi during his 1986 run for President of Austria (which he won).

Wall Street Gerbil: The *Wall Street Journal* newspaper.

to Wig: To go crazy; to get angry.

Wig city: A mental hospital.

Wiggy: Crazy.

Yom Kippur Clipper: A Jewish Cadillac that stops on a dime and picks it up.

LOTTIE'S LOVE

When Lottie Cotton was born, on September 6, 1902, in the tiny southeast Texas town of Liberty, there were no airplanes in the sky. There were no SUVs, no superhighways, no cell phones, no televisions. When Lottie was laid to rest in Houston, there was a black Jesus looking after her from the wall of the funeral chapel. Many biblical scholars agree today that Jesus, being of North African descent, very likely may have been black. But Lottie was always spiritually color-blind; her Jesus was the color of love. She spent her entire life looking after others. One of them, I'm privileged to say, was me.

Lottie was not a maid. She was not a nanny. She did not live with us. We were not rich rug rats raised in River Oaks. We lived in a middle-class neighborhood of Houston. My mother was one of the first speech therapists hired by the Houston Independent School District; my father traveled throughout the Southwest doing community-relations work. Lottie helped cook and baby-sit during the day and soon became part of our family.

I was old enough to realize yet young enough to know that I was in the presence of a special person. Laura Bush, my occasional pen pal, had this to say about Lottie in a recent letter, and I don't think she'd mind my sharing it with you: "Only special ladies earn the title of 'second mother.' She must have been a remarkable person, and I know you miss her."

> **Lottie was always spiritually color-blind; her Jesus was the color of love.**

There are not many people like Lottie left in this world. Few of us, indeed, have the time and the love to spend our days and nights looking after others. Most of us take our responsibilities to our own families seriously. Many of us work hard at our jobs. Some of us even do unto others as we would have them do unto us. But how many would freely, willingly, lovingly roam the cotton fields of the heart with two young boys and a young girl, a cocker spaniel named Rex, and a white mouse named Archimedes?

One way or another for almost fifty-five years, wherever I traveled in the world, Lottie and I managed to stay in touch. I now calculate that when Lottie sent me birthday cards in Borneo when I was in the Peace Corps, she was in her early sixties, an age that I myself am now rapidly, if disbelievingly, approaching. She also remained in touch with my brother,

Roger, who lives in Maryland, and my sister, Marcie, who lives in Vietnam. To live a hundred years on this troubled planet is a rare feat, but to maintain contact with your "children" for all that length of time, and for them to have become your dear friends in later years, is rarer still.

For Lottie did not survive one century in merely the clinical sense; she was as sharp as a tack until the end of her days. At the ripe young age of ninety-nine, she could sit at the kitchen table and discuss politics or religion—or stuffed animals. Lottie left behind an entire menagerie of teddy bears and other stuffed animals, each of them with a name and personality all its own. She also left behind two live animals, dogs named Minnie and Little Dog, who had followed her and protected her everywhere she went. Minnie is a little dog named for my mother, and Little Dog, as might be expected, is a big dog.

Was it too late, I wondered, to bless the hands that prepared the food?

Yours is the immortality of a precious passenger on the train to glory, which has taken you from the cross ties on the railroad to the stars in the sky.

Lottie is survived by her daughter, Ada Beverly (the two of them have referred to each other as "Mama" for at least the past thirty years) and one grandson, Jeffery. She's also survived by Roger, Marcie, and me, who live scattered about a modern-day world, a world that has gained so much in technology yet seems to have lost those sacred recipes for popcorn balls and chocolate-chip cookies. "She was a seasoned saint," a young preacher who had never met her said at her funeral. But was it too late, I wondered, to bless the hands that prepared the food? And there were so many other talents in Lottie's gentle hands, not the least of which was the skill to be a true mender of the human spirit.

I don't know what else you can say about someone who has been in your life forever, someone who was always there for you, even when "there" was far away. Lottie was my mother's friend, she was my friend, and now she has a friend in Jesus. She always had a friend in Jesus, come to think of it. The foundation of her faith was as strong as the foundation for the railroad tracks she helped lay as a young girl in Liberty. Lottie, you've outlived your very bones, darling. Yours is not the narrow immortality craved by the authors, actors, and artists

of this world. Yours is the immortality of a precious passenger on the train to glory, which has taken you from the cross ties on the railroad to the stars in the sky.

By day and by night, each in their turn, the sun and the moon gaze through the window, now and again reflecting upon the gold and silver pathways of childhood. The pathways are still there, but we cannot see them with our eyes, nor shall we ever again tread lightly upon them with our feet. Yet as children, we never suspect we might someday lose our way. We think we have all the time in the world.

I am still here, Lottie. And Ada gave me two of the teddy bears that I sent you long ago. As I write these words, those bears sit on the windowsill looking after me. Some might say they are only stuffed animals. But, Lottie, you and I know what's really inside them. It's the stuff of dreams.